DISCARDED

What?!
ANOTHER NEW MANDATE?

This book is dedicated to my two loves—my husband
Bryan and daughter Blair.

What?!
ANOTHER NEW MANDATE?
WHAT AWARD-WINNING
TEACHERS DO WHEN SCHOOL RULES CHANGE

Randi Stone

CORWIN PRESS, INC.
A Sage Publications Company
Thousand Oaks, California

For information:

Corwin Press, Inc.
A Sage Publications Company
2455 Teller Road
Thousand Oaks, California 91320
www.corwinpress.com

Sage Publications Ltd.
6 Bonhill Street
London EC2A 4PU
United Kingdom

Sage Publications India Pvt. Ltd.
M-32 Market
Greater Kailash I
New Delhi 110 048 India

Printed in the United States of America

Library of Congress Cataloging-in-Publication Data

What?! Another new mandate? : What award-winning teachers do when school rules change / [edited by] Randi Stone.
     p. cm.
Includes index.
 ISBN 0-7619-4504-0 – ISBN 0-7619-4505-9 (pbk.)
 1. Teacher effectiveness—United States—Anecdotes. 2. Educational change—United States—Anecdotes. I. Stone, Randi.
LB1775.2 .W46 2003
371.1–dc21
                                        2002010379

This book is printed on acid-free paper.

02 03 04 05 06 07 7 6 5 4 3 2 1

Acquisitions Editor:	Faye Zucker
Editorial Assistant:	Julia Parnell
Copy Editor:	Toni Williams
Production Editor:	Olivia Weber
Typesetter/Designer:	C&M Digitals (P) Ltd
Indexer:	Michael Ferreira
Cover Designer:	Tracy E. Miller
Production Artist:	Michelle Lee

Contents

Preface

I t seems the phrase that most accurately describes education is "ever changing." This book surveys award-winning
teachers around the country about changes in their classrooms and their coping strategies.

Topics range from how technology has changed learning
to the advent of state standards and mandated testing. One
thing, however, has not changed and that's the willingness of
teachers to share—to share their knowledge.

September 11, 2001, changed us all. I would like for you to
experience the heartfelt words from teachers regarding how
they handled that day. Read how teachers reacted when many
pairs of questioning eyes looked to them for guidance.

WHO SHOULD READ THIS BOOK

This book is for K-12 educators. Change happens across the
board, whether it's at the elementary, middle school, or high
school level. This book could also be a resource for administrators interested in seeing what award-winning educators are
doing to cope with changes in education.

ACKNOWLEDGMENTS

I thank all the extraordinary teaches across the country who
shared their insights. Grateful acknowledgment is also made
to the contributors for special permission to use their material.
All rights are reserved.

About the Author

Randi Stone is a graduate of Clark University, Boston University, and Salem State College. She holds credentials for elementary education and a master of science in broadcast communication. She completed her EdD at the University of Massachusetts, Lowell. She is the author of previous books with Corwin Press including *New Ways to Teach Using Cable Television: A Step-by-Step Guide* and *Best Practices for High School Classrooms: What Award-Winning Secondary Teachers Do.* Her publication *Best Classroom Practices: What Award-Winning Elementary Teachers Do* is a best-seller.

About the Contributors

Cindy Albert, Foreign Language Teacher
Hilltop School
19 Marshall Avenue
Caribou, Maine 04736
School Telephone Number: (207) 493-4250
E-mail: calbert@mail.caribou.k12.me.us
Number of Years Teaching: 9
Awards: 2000 Milken Educator, 2000
National Board Certified, Early Childhood Generalist, 1999
MSAD #20 Teacher of the Year, 1996-1997

Kimberly Allen, Assistant Principal
Montebello School
5725 North 27th Avenue
Phoenix, Arizona 85017
School Telephone Number: (602) 336-2000
E-mail: kallen@alhambra.k12.az.us
Awards: Milken Family Foundation National Educator
    Award, 2000
Appointment to Governor's Commission on Civil Rights,
    2000-2003
Golden Bell Award, Arizona School Board Association, 1999

Claude Jean Archer, Former Fourth and Fifth Grade Teacher,
    Instructional Staffing Officer
Miami Dade County Public Schools

14262 SW 90 Terrace
Miami, Florida 33186
School Telephone Number: (305) 995-7225
E-mail: carcher@bellsouth.net
Number of Years Teaching: 10
Awards: Milken Family Foundation National Educator
    Award, 2000
National Board Certification, Exceptional Needs
    Specialist, 2000
Teacher of the Year, Marjory Stoneman Douglas
    Elementary, 2000

Avalyn Balliet, Social Studies Department Chair,
    Eighth Grade U.S. History Teacher
Austin Middle School
825 E. Union Bower Road
Irving, Texas 75061
School Telephone Number: (972) 721-3100
E-mail: avisballiet@yahoo.com
Number of Years Teaching: 7
Awards: Milken Family Foundation National Educator
    Award, 2000
Irving Independent School District Secondary Teacher of the
    Year, 2000
Austin Middle School Campus Teacher of the Year, 2000

Lloyd Barber, First Grade Teacher
Kingsley Elementary
2300 Green Bay Road
Evanston, Illinois 60201
School Telephone Number: (847) 492-5969
E-mail: third205@aol.com
Number of Years Teaching: 20+
Awards: Red Apple Teaching Award, 2000
Kohl/McCormick Early Childhood Teaching
    Award, 1999
Fellowship Award, American Antiquarian Society, 1995

Susan L.Barr, Fourth Grade Teacher
Narragansett Elementary
55 Mumford Road
Narragansett, Rhode Island 02882
School Telephone Number: (401) 792-9420
E-mail: ride3456@ride.ri.net
Number of Years Teaching: 22
Awards: NBPTS Early Childhood Generalist, November 2000

James M. Brown, Sixth Grade Teacher
Lisha Kill Middle School
68 Waterman Avenue
Albany, New York 12205
School Telephone Number: (518) 456-2306
E-mail: jmbrown@nycap.rr.com
Number of Years Teaching: 8
Awards: Drug, Chemical, and Allied Trades Association
    Education Foundation's "Making a Difference" Award,
    January 2001
New York State Lottery's "Educator of the Week,"
    November 2000
Toyota Tapestry Award, January 1998

Vincent Carbone, Jr., Science Lead Teacher
North Stratfield School
190 Putting Green Road
Fairfield, Connecticut 06432
School Telephone Number: (203) 255-8322
E-mail: vcnss@yahoo.com
Number of Years Teaching: 12
Awards: NSTA 2001 Barrick Goldstrike Exemplary
    Elementary Earth Science Teaching Award
Council for Elementary Science International Muriel Green
    Award, 1992

Lynn L. Clark, Third-Fourth Grade Teacher
Liberty School

9332 Hwy. 36
Joes, Colorado 80822
School Telephone Number: (970) 358-4288
E-mail: clarkgreenll@yahoo.com
Number of Years Teaching: 15
Awards: Ernest Duncan Grant, National Council of Teachers
    of Mathematics, April 2001

Colleen Cooper, Fifth Grade Teacher, Codirector of Montana
    Abacus Institute
Hellgate Elementary
2385 Flynn Lane
Missoula, Montana 59808
School Telephone Number: (406) 549-6109
E-mail: ccooper@hellgate.k12.mt.us
Number of years Teaching: 20
Awards: Milken Family Foundation National Educator
    Award, 2000
Montana Teacher of the Year Finalist, 1998
Wal-Mart Teacher of the Year, 1998

MaryEllen Daneels, Social Studies Teacher and Teacher for
    Alternative Educational Program
Community High School
326 Joliet Street
West Chicago, Illinois 60185
School Telephone Number: (630) 876-6453
E-mail: mdaneels@juno.com
Number of Years Teaching: 11
Awards: Class Webpage, MidLink Magazine, Honor Roll of
    A+ Best Web Sites.
Chosen to be State Coordinator for the Dirksen Congressional
    Center to Promote Civic Education.
Who's Who Among America's High School Teachers,
    1990-present

Kristen Dewitt, Teacher
Cooper Elementary School

7559 N. 14th St.
Kalamazoo, Michigan 49009
School Telephone Number: (616) 349-2674
E-mail: kdewitt@plainwellschools.org
Number of Years Teaching: 11
Awards: National Board for Professional Teaching Standards
    Recipient, November 2000
Plainwell Community Schools, Employee Merit Award
    Recipient, October 2000

Carmella E. Ettaro, Math Chair
Westlake High School
100 N. Lakeview Canyon Road
Westlake Village, California 91362
School Telephone Number: (805) 497-6711
E-mail: coratte@aol.com
Number of Years Teaching: 31
Awards: State Farm Good Neighbor Award, March 2001
Honorary Service and Continuing Service Award, 2000
Honored Teacher Recognition by California Credentialing
    Commission and Governor's Office, 1994

Gerald Friday, Biology Teacher
Marquette High School
3401 W. Wisconsin Ave.
Milwaukee, Wisconsin 53208
School Telephone Number: (414) 933-7220
E-mail: friday@muhs.edu
Number of Years Teaching: 37
Awards (Past five years): Teacher of the Year, Department of
    Natural Resources
Teacher of the Year, Wisconsin Association of Environmental
    Education
Teacher of the Year, American Entomological Society

Allison G. Gregerson, Teacher
T. Roosevelt Middle School
3315 Maine Avenue

Kenner, Louisiana 70065
School Telephone Number: (504) 443-1361
E-mail: caj02@juno.com
Number of Years Teaching: 11.5
Awards: Dale Seymour Scholarship, 2001
Quality Science and Math Grant Recipient, 1995, 1998
S. Worley Jr. High Teacher of the Year, 1995

Mary E. Harris, Chemistry Teacher
John Burroughs School
755 South Price Road
St. Louis, Missouri 63124
School Telephone Number: (314) 993-4040
E-mail: mharris@jburroughs.org
Number of Years Teaching: 29
Awards: Gustav Ohaus Award for Innovation in Science
    Teaching, First Place, 2001
Missouri State Finalist for the Presidential Award for
    Excellence in Secondary Science Teaching, 2000, 2001
ExploraVision National Awards with my students,
    1997, 1998, 1999

Percy Hill, Health and Physical Education Teacher
Andover Elementary/Middle School
Main Street
Andover, New Hampshire 03216
School Telephone Number: (603) 735-5494 or 5400
E-mail: dolfin@tds.net
Number of Years Teaching: 29
Awards: Disney American Teacher Award Honoree, 2000
National Association of Sport and Physical Education Teacher
    of the Year, New Hampshire, 1999
New Hampshire Association of Health, Physical Education,
    Recreation and Dance Middle School Teacher of the
    Year, 1997

Steven T. Jackson, Principal
Spotswood Elementary School

400 Mountain View Drive
Harrisonburg, Virginia 22801
School Telephone Number: (540) 434-3429
E-mail: sjackson@harrisburg.k12.va.us
Awards: Milken Educator Award, 2000

Sharon Jeffery, Science Teacher, NBCT in Early
    Adolescent Science
Plymouth South Middle School
488 Long Pond Road
Plymouth, Massachusetts 02360
School Telephone Number: (508) 224-2725
E-mail: sjeffery@plymouth.k12.ma.us
Number of Years Teaching: 22
Awards: National Board for Professional Teaching Standards,
    Certified in Early Adolescence Science, 1999
Environmental Award from the Massachusetts
    Environmental Secretary for a Curriculum on
    Water Conservation, 1998

Lynn Rylander Kaufman, Fourth Grade Teacher
Hillside Elementary
7500 Western Avenue
Omaha, Nebraska 68114
School Telephone Number: (402) 390-6450
E-mail: lkaufman@westside66.org
Number of Years Teaching: 25+
Awards: National Board Certification
Milken Educator Award
Nebraska State Teacher of the Year

Caryn Smith Long, Science and Technology Facilitator
Winterfield Elementary School
3100 Winterfield Place
Charlotte, North Carolina 28205
School Telephone Number: (704) 343-6400
E-mail: edupro@juno.com
Number of Years Teaching: 13

Awards: National Science Teacher's Association,
    Distinguished Teaching Award, March 2001
Presidential Award for Excellence in Math and Science
    Teaching, Elementary Science, March 2001
American Association of University Women, Eleanor
    Roosevelt Teaching Fellowship, June 1999

Michelle C. Mash, Kindergarten Teacher
2653 Whitman Drive
Wilmington, Delaware 19808
School Telephone Number: (302) 636-5681
E-mail: smm34@infi.net
Number of Years Teaching: 13
Awards: National Board Certified Teacher, 2000
MBNA Most Innovative Grant Award, 2000
Nominee for Building Teacher of the Year, 1999

Jeff McAdoo, Physical Education Teacher
Quail Run Elementary School
Lawrence, Kansas 66067
School Telephone Number: (785) 832-5820
E-mail: jmcadoo@usd497.org
Number of Years Teaching: 17
Awards: Emporia State University, School of Education
    "Outstanding Recent Graduate," 2001
Milken Family Foundation National Educator, 2000
Elementary Teacher of the Year, Lawrence, Kansas,
    USD497, 2000

Rosalyn L. Pollard, Teacher Consultant
Stevenson Middle School
38501 Palmer Road
Westland, Michigan 48185
School Telephone Number: (734) 595-2500
E-mail: pollardrl@aol.com
Number of Years Teaching: 24
Awards: Wayne-Westland Way to Go, Winter 2000
National Board Certified Teacher, November 2000

Karen Quillen, Math Teacher
Sumner High School
1701 Main Street
Sumner, Washington 98390
School Telephone Number: (253) 891-5500
E-mail: Karen_quillen@sumner.wednet.edu
Number of Years Teaching: 20+
Awards: SHS Teacher of the Year, 1991-1995
Air Force Certificate of Appreciation for Outstanding
    Support and Dedication to Ideals and Principals of the
    United States of America
Phi Kappa Phi, National Honor Society

Erika Reynolds, Kindergarten Teacher, National Board
    Certified Teacher
Arlington Elementary
3511 Arlington Street
Pascagoula, Mississippi 39581
School Telephone Number: (228) 938-6552
E-mail: ereynolds@pascagoula.k12.ms.us
Number of Years Teaching: 11
Awards: National Board Certification, Early Childhood
    Generalist, November 1999
Alabama Economic Teacher of the Year State Finalist, 1998
TSPAT Scholar, Technology Scholarship Recipient of
    Technology Scholarship Through the State

Peter W. Riffle, Learning Support Teacher
Wilson High School
2601 Grandview Boulevard
West Lawn, Pennsylvania 19609
School Telephone Number: (610) 670-0185
Number of Years Teaching: 33
Awards: Disney American Teacher Award Honoree, 2000

Linda Seeger, Mathematics Instructor
Okoboji High School
907 H Avenue

Milford, Iowa 51351
School Telephone Number: (712) 388-2446
E-mail: lseeger@okoboji.k12.ia.us
Number of Years Teaching: 15
Awards: National Board Certification in Adolescence and
   Young Adult Mathematics, November 1999

Luis R. Soria, National Board Certified Teacher
Augustus H. Burley
1630 W. Barry
Chicago, Illinois 60657
School Telephone Number: (773) 534-5475
E-mail: soriarush@earthlink.net
Number of Years Teaching: 8
Awards: Kohl/McCormick Early Childhood
   Teaching Award, 2000
Chicago Foundation for Education Award, 2000
Rochelle Lee Fund Award, 2000

Kay Wallace, Math Teacher
Pickerington High School
300 Opportunity Way
Pickerington, Ohio 43147
School Telephone Number: (614) 833-3025
E-mail: kayIWallace@aol.com
Number of Years Teaching: 28
Awards: Radio Shack National Teacher Award, 2001
Presidential Award for Excellence in Math and Science
   Teaching (State Level), 2000
Toyota's Investment in Math Education, 1998

Teachers Staying on Top of Changes

Professional Development Has Shaped Me and My Classroom

KAY WALLACE

Pickerington, Ohio

It is no secret that professional development requirements and opportunities have increased over the past several years. In Ohio, the new teaching license requirements call for a certain number of contact or credit hours of professional development for each license renewal, and teachers must continue this process throughout their tenure.

The state also requires all teachers to write and follow an individual professional development plan to help teachers focus those professional experiences toward something that will be of value to them. In addition, the state has channeled monies to the regional professional development centers to provide many meaningful offerings and opportunities for the teaching profession.

Teachers should embrace this change and take advantage of the many opportunities that were not there even five years ago. There are some marvelous vehicles that allow teachers to grow and classroom instruction to improve. Six years ago I began teaching an integrated algebra and chemistry course which has led me to many such opportunities.

Once I began teaching this integration of disciplines and could write about the new and exciting things that were happening in my classroom, I received many grants and awards for innovative teaching practices. These awards not only provided supplies and equipment, but almost always allowed for professional development as well.

The corporations and organizations giving these awards saw the necessity and value of professional development. This allowed me the opportunity to take classes and to travel to workshops and conferences to learn more ways to change and improve my curriculum and classroom practices. This has been invaluable to me in both creating excitement among the students and growing as a teacher.

While I am still refreshing and improving classroom practices, others have invited my teaching partner and me to share with them what we have learned from our day-to-day teaching and from others. We have presented conference sessions, workshops, and classes on integrating math and science, integrating several disciplines with thematic units, and using technology for data analysis. It is always a pleasure to meet with other teachers, share ideas, and connect professionally. This has been a growing experience for me and has allowed me to build a cadre of professional colleagues who help me continue to grow and who provide support.

I am also involved with our regional mentoring program. I provide training for teachers to be mentors to new entry-year teachers as well as serve as a mentor myself. This program has caused me to look at the teaching and learning in my classroom, to reflect upon my practices, and to grow from this experience as well.

Another role I have played in professional development is to help plan workshops and classes for teachers in my area. I am a member of our Regional Professional Development Board, and our primary role is to plan professional development opportunities for teachers in the southeast region of the state. It has been very rewarding to discover teachers' needs in professional development and to facilitate these offerings.

I also serve on the board of the Ohio Council of Teachers of Mathematics, and there again I look at professional development opportunities in the form of workshops or our state conference. I am also on the committee for the council's state teaching awards, which is another opportunity for teachers. What an exciting time to be a teacher, with all of these opportunities for improvement at your fingertips!

Yes, professional development takes time in planning, attending, and implementing, but it is time well spent. There are so many more exciting opportunities for teachers today; you cannot afford to miss out. Professional development improves instruction, often changes the focus from curriculum to how children learn, and definitely enlivens the teacher. You owe it to yourself and your students to take the time to recharge and embrace change.

Helpful Tips

Time is often a problem for teachers. During any given week, I might find myself working on a grant, planning to teach a workshop, and attending meetings, as well as planning and grading for my classes. I could easily find myself bogged down if I kept looking at everything that had to be done. Learn to prioritize. Decide what must get done today, and concentrate only on that project. When that is finished, decide what must be done next. And please remember, every project is worthwhile and rewarding.

Teachers Go Back to School

STEVEN T. JACKSON

Harrisonburg, Virginia

Spotswood Elementary School is located in Harrisonburg, Virginia. We are a small college town located in the Shenandoah Valley. Our school contains Grades K-5 and houses just over 400 students. Our class size is 17.5 and there are four sections within each grade level.

We have a focus on early childhood education with two Head Start classes, three early childhood special education classes, and one preschool autistic class. Typically, these students become integrated into our kindergarten classes. Sixty-two percent of our students come from impoverished homes. Almost 40% come from homes where English is not the primary language spoken. Spanish, Kurdish, and Russian are our three most spoken languages after English.

Virginia is a high-stakes testing state. The Virginia Standards of Learning (SOLs) provide a framework for K-12 education within our state. The intent of the SOLs is to provide clear, basic academic goals. These standards are then tested in Grades 3, 5, and 8 and designated courses in high school. School accreditation is directly tied to student pass rates (most at the 70% level) on these tests.

As an elementary school in the state of Virginia, our mission is to prepare our students for testing at Grades 3 and 5. Our faculty brainstormed strategies for improving student performance on these tests. One thread ran through the discussion: literacy.

We all know that for students to perform well, they must be literate and able to read the test. As in most schools, our upper elementary teachers really did not have any idea of what our primary teachers deal with academically. The feeling was reciprocated with primary teachers.

The idea of creating a literacy course grew from these discussions. The course was a three-hour graduate credit offering from Eastern Mennonite University. The schedule for the course lasted all year. Some classes were held after school, while others were a Friday night, Saturday morning combination. All teachers within the school were required to attend the course. As an instructional leader, I am not typically a tyrannical ogre. In this case, however, I found it necessary to be just that. There would not be any teachers missing this opportunity!

As the class got under way, a few themes became prevalent: (1) teachers should have a larger block of unencumbered time in which to teach language arts, (2) each classroom has a wonderful array of books and literacy materials which we should bring all together, and (3) literacy should be the basis for all other learning.

A group of staff members worked on the 2000-2001 schedule to achieve the first theme. Teachers have reported that they are better equipped timewise to teach a complete language arts block. Another group of teachers created guidelines for our new book room. All teachers donated their classroom sets of books and during the summer, each title was leveled. Now we have thousands of books in one location from levels 0 to 60. Teachers have been supplied with a complete list of every title. When teachers need to use any of the titles, they merely check them out on a computer dedicated to this purpose.

Our book room has been used as a model for other schools considering the same type of change. Having this available for our teachers also allows us to use literacy funds more wisely. It becomes very evident where our weaknesses lie and what reading levels need to be bolstered.

Teachers infuse the knowledge learned from this solution every day with every lesson they teach. Word study groups and literature circles are commonplace. Word walls have replaced the traditional bulletin boards. Classes K-5 concentrate on journaling. Students read their journals and latest books to the principal and assistant principal. Our Title I reading specialists, English as a Second Language teachers, and classroom instructors collaborate to provide small journaling groups in the primary grades. At the third, fourth, and fifth grade levels, they provide small-group literature circles using trade books to teach reading.

Perhaps the greatest outcome of this literacy class was a schoolwide feeling that we are making and will continue to make a huge difference among the children we serve. As state-mandated testing looms at the third and fifth grades every spring, we are confident that our children will be literate enough to be able to read and understand the tests. Teachers and administrators throughout Virginia are constantly trying to devise new ways to prepare their students. We believe literacy is the key.

Keeping Up With Change

CARYN SMITH LONG

Charlotte, North Carolina

Flexibility is the key to survival in this profession. This is the one thing that I share at the beginning of each of my college classes that I teach at UNC-Charlotte and what I would like to tell some of my colleagues. The field of education is a constantly evolving one and any good teacher will tell you that you must keep up with current trends in education in order to serve children in the best manner possible.

Taking advantage of school system workshops is probably the most common way in which teachers avail themselves of changes in education. It is also the weakest way to keep up with new trends and studies, as workshops tend to be run by professionals who are not always privy to or willing to avail themselves of the latest educational research.

Instead, they are disseminators of such information or they are simply told what to do but not allowed to use their own creativity to share their learned information. Also, most school-system-offered courses are mandated by the school system or state and are not necessarily ones in which teachers are clamoring to enroll. Too often, negative attitudes prevail in these sessions and the negativity passes over the participants like a tidal wave.

There are two things that I do to keep myself aware of the changes in curriculum and instruction in our state. First, I work with local colleges to mentor future teachers. These students are at the forefront of current knowledge regarding changes in education: our universities.

Colleges of education must always be apprised of new trends so they can prepare their students for the workforce. I find when I teach a course at the university or when I mentor new teachers, I learn as much from them as they do from me.

Second, as teachers, it is part of our job to become involved in every aspect of education. This means using as much of our spare time as possible to participate in local initiatives that educate us about new curriculum changes. When studies from Japan arrived in the United States regarding constructivist theories of education, local science leaders presented the information to our school system. I felt a connection to this teaching method and made myself available to presenting workshops about constructivism and the discovery methods of teaching.

From this involvement, I was given further information about these new emerging theories through training initiatives for those of us who were involved in training other teachers. Over the years, as my expertise grew, my involvement with this local initiative caused a domino effect. Doors open when you make yourself available to opportunities that extend your own knowledge.

Philosophies
of Change

Self-Reflection: Looking
Over Your Own Shoulder

SUSAN BARR

Narragansett, Rhode Island

The most exhilarating, yet at the same time frustrating aspect of being a teacher is the comprehensiveness of it all. Contributing to the comprehensiveness are two important variable categories I call the *players* and the *rules* of the profession.

The players are the children, teachers, parents, staff members, administration, teacher unions, school committees, town councils, state department officials, national education officials, and so-called experts in the field. The rules include grade-level outcomes and expectations, standardized tests, mandated curricula and programs, student assessments, and teacher evaluations. In addition, these variables are likely to change at any time. In the case of my classroom, I have 20 "variables" whose needs change every single day!

Professional development in the form of coursework, inservice workshops, and research can be helpful. The opportunity to engage in professional collaboration and conversation with my colleagues has always proven to be beneficial, but I believe the most powerful endeavor has been engaging in self-reflective questioning. Without this component, much of the above-mentioned efforts lose their significance.

The period of time I reflect on ranges from what occurred during the past ten minutes to what occurred during the past school year. I ask myself these questions: Did things go the way I expected them to go? Were the outcomes met? How can I improve or enrich the experience next time? Were different learning styles addressed? Were the children engaged in the process? What resources can I tap that will help me achieve my goal?

Self-reflection and questioning, while very rewarding, can admittedly be uncomfortable and even disturbing. There is an element of uneasiness at times, a feeling of rocking the boat. Viewing myself as an evolving person and professional affords me the luxury of being imperfect. We all make mistakes. Self-reflection allows us to see those mistakes, fine-tune our actions, and move forward. I suggest four basic tenets as a guide:

1. Take small steps

2. Remain cautious and guard the tried and true, yet be adventurous enough to explore new options

3. Be flexible

4. Trust your instincts

As I gain experience in the field of education, the work actually appears to be more complex and challenging now than it was when I was a novice teacher over 20 years ago. Becoming a self-reflective practitioner has allowed me to continue to do the work that I love with a feeling of renewed dedication, commitment, enthusiasm, and enjoyment.

Change Doesn't Have to Hurt

ALLISON GREGERSON

Kenner, Louisiana

C hange! Say this word to any senior veteran of our faculty and eyes will roll. The word *change* strikes fear into the hearts of many teachers. We have been asked to change the way we teach our classes, how we view our students, how we discipline our students, how we develop our lessons, and even what we teach.

Teachers are constantly being asked to try something new. "I have this great new program I think we should try," our principal says, and you can hear the "Oh no, not another one" wave around the room. Somehow, though, those of us who have committed ourselves to changing with the times take the new program, implement a little bit of it, and say, "Oh, yes, this works great," just to please our principal.

The point is that change doesn't have to hurt. The basic idea of change is that you should change 10% of what you do each year. When I learned about using manipulatives in the math classroom, I was scared of letting go of my always-silent classroom. With manipulatives and self-exploration come lots and lots of talking, disagreements, and yes, laughter. I wasn't ready for the noise level. I took one lesson we learned at our workshop, a lesson on introducing integers, and tried it. The students really enjoyed it and participated more. They even had more right answers and could explain themselves better. This excited me. I thought, "Hey, this is great. Maybe I'll try another one." I did, with pleasing results.

As one great lesson turned into another, I found myself trying to find, and create, more and more fun lessons for the students. I wanted them to participate and learn, and they wanted to participate and learn. There was a time I never thought we would desire the same goals, but it was starting to happen.

This past year, as I became more comfortable with our standards, textbook, and high-stakes testing, I threw out the textbook and taught strictly from teacher-created exploratory activities. They loved finding the circumference of circles by measuring paper plates, toilet paper rolls, Crystal Light containers, and whatever other circular items I could gather. They had to measure at least three in order to begin to see a pattern develop. They loved going on a treasure hunt with their rulers, yardsticks or metersticks, and charts to find hidden objects within the school to measure.

They loved learning how to differentiate between positive and negative numbers using red and white beans. By using activities, they could see where the meaning of math was beginning to come together. When our high-stakes testing came around, I wasn't as confident as I should have been because I did find many students not completing the activities, but they surprised me. Osmosis took over, and just listening to their friends and group members, and having to participate, helped them to learn more than I thought. It was the doing that helped them remember the strategies and applications.

I did have to implement *group rules*, such as "You must use an 18-inch voice when working in your groups," not only to reinforce how closely they were working, but also because it's mathematical and they need to understand the 18-inch concept. I also have posted the group rules. They realize quickly that if they start discussing subjects other than the one at hand, then it can be the cause for extra assignments.

This usually keeps them on task, in addition to the fact that they eventually want to be the first group to figure out the correct answer. Group work is something that you have to try once, evaluate, make corrections, and try again. It is a never-ending cycle that you are constantly working to perfect as each group tries the activity. Eventually, they learn what is expected of them.

I can't say that I still don't roll my eyes, reject new ideas that my principal presents, and go home and scream, "I can't believe they want me to do this!" I can say that by applying my 10% rule, it has made my life, classroom, and changes more manageable, and I find myself more willing to try these new changes and standards. It's never perfect, but at least now we have fun trying, making mistakes, and learning. My students are more responsive and active participants because I'm willing to make learning fun and exciting.

I Am a Teacher and
I Would Be None Other

LYNN KAUFMAN

Omaha, Nebraska

Seven years ago my next teaching assignment was a dream come true—a brand-new, upscale suburban school with dedicated, energetic colleagues and an outstanding principal with a vision of excellence. My stint as State Teacher of the Year was ending, and I was anxious to refocus my efforts and energy toward teaching and my classroom. I was on top of the world, ready for anything.

Together, we—teachers, principal, and staff—forged a school that would become second to none. We came early, stayed late, and loved every moment. We walked around ladders, unpacked hundreds of boxes, sloshed through floods in the teachers' lounge, and spent hours building programs, schedules, and friendships.

I was assigned first grade—my favorite level—so it seemed the perfect place to finish my career. On the first day of class I took a deep breath and inhaled the newness of our beautiful school. I mused, could teaching get any better?

At some point during that first year a small, niggling rash of discontent began growing on my spirit. I was perplexed because I could not identify the source of my discontent. I searched my personal and professional life and found no answers. I subscribe to the adage "For things to change, you have to change." I sought change to relieve the itch. During the next five years, change was my middle name.

The second year my friend and I started a multiage second and third grade primary center with 48 students. Between us we had more than 25 years of teaching experience and were quite confident about success. We spent the summer planning instruction and designing and arranging the environment in our classroom.

When the children arrived they walked into a beautiful room filled with tables, pillows and comfy furniture, plants, fish tanks, live animals and birds, thousands of books, wonderful works of art, and a science center laden with an array of specimens and gadgets to explore.

They also walked in with 96 boxes of tissue, 960 pencils, 240 folders, 144 notebooks, 48 backpacks, and all sizes and sorts of Trapper Keepers. My colleague and I looked at each other and paled. We had forgotten to leave room for supplies in our beautiful environment!

When lunchtime rolled around, we missed our cafeteria time; we couldn't see the clock behind the stacks of 96 tissue boxes. As we frantically tried to distribute cold lunches and hot lunch tickets, we suddenly realized that we had no system in place for lunch routines or for lining up to leave the classroom. That day we had to beg the cooks' forgiveness, but no one went hungry.

After school, when the principal came in to check how our first day had gone, he found us lying on the floor faint with fatigue, laughter, and tears. The primary center existed for two years and then closed because the school shifted from multiage to looping classrooms where we kept an entire class for two years. To this day, the primary center remains the most consuming, exciting, and exhilarating teaching experience of my career. During those two years, my niggling rash of discontent did not grow, but it also did not fade. I just ignored the itch.

During our second year in the primary center I was named a Milken Educator. For several months I was caught up in the swirl of the honor and all the expectations associated with a national-level award. Later that summer, as I waited silently in the wings backstage to receive my $25,000, I reflected about why I was there.

My mind wandered back 10 years as I sifted through stories of those special children none of us ever forget. I thought about a belligerent, low-achieving little boy. He solved his problems first with foul language and then with fists and feet. The battered child of a broken home and an alcoholic parent, he knew he was unlovable. Some days I had agreed.

I rarely kept student notes, but still had one from him: "I am special to me and you are special. I like you. I love you. I like school." This eight-year-old taught me things about learning and living that I will never forget. I knew when I mounted the steps into the spotlight that the stories of all those children like him were with me.

During the next two years I looped with my first grade to second grade. This was truly one of the brightest and most dynamic classes of my career. Fourteen of 21 students were identified as gifted, and I found myself scrambling to keep ahead of them. The MA in gifted education that I had completed two years earlier did not prepare me for the level of learning these children needed and demanded. Every day presented new and exciting opportunities.

Sometime during those years I began to notice several subtle, unsought changes. On many mornings when I pulled into the school parking lot, I found myself repeating the same litany, "I can and I will, I can and I will." *Retirement* and *weekend* were frequent words in my vocabulary, and I realized that I was tired and disheartened. Despite all the honors, the unique and exhilarating changes I had made, the wonderful class I was teaching, and the school of my dreams, I felt my joy of teaching fading and my spirit sagging.

One day I reread some of my own words and was struck by what I had written seven years before: "I have watched the light of understanding illuminate a girl's face, but held a child as authorities questioned him about the bruises on his body. I have applauded the production of a young playwright and wept as I read the poignant verse of a young poet. I have restrained a child as he tried to harm himself and have seen a life changed when a child—who thought herself without intelligence—discovered that she could read. I am a teacher and I would be none other." Lately, I was not so sure that I wanted to be "none other."

The following year, because of staffing needs, I was assigned to a fourth grade looping to fifth grade. History and the prairie fascinate me so I was eager to plunge into the new curriculum. I thought the opportunity to tackle new content might quell my growing discontent. My new teaching team was the strongest in the school and I found myself laughing, enjoying, and learning. But still the niggling rash and itch persisted.

I decided to seek National Board Teacher Certification. The structure and process, which is very intense and personal, forced me to reflect on the teacher I had been, the teacher I was, and the teacher I could become. What I saw was a teacher with little purpose and less initiative. What I wanted was to return to myself: "I am a teacher and I would be none other." I just did not know how to make that happen in that context.

Then one day, everything changed. My class and I were discussing poverty and how we could make a difference in the world. As we talked, several students shared their personal images of poverty. One student shared his memories of visiting New Delhi where he walked in crowded streets and dodged begging children. Another student gave a moving and poignant description of ragged children and smelly outhouses she had seen in the Bahamas. An outhouse discussion in the fourth grade always supersedes a poverty discussion.

As they talked, I scanned my students and realized every one of them lived in a house with at least three bathrooms! It was then that I recognized the cause of my discontent and knew the kind of salve needed for my spirit. I needed more stories.

One month into the process, I decided to seek a teaching position at an urban Title I school in a neighboring district.

Even though my principal and I understood that this was a decision of the spirit and not of the situation, we both experienced profound loss. This school—the children, parents, and my colleagues—had a hold on me that would last forever, and I knew the change would be the toughest of my career. I pressed onward.

During my interview I told the new principal that I did not have any significant "stories" and I needed to be in a place where there were lots of them. He assured me there would be no shortage of stories at this school. Two months later, four strong young men loaded 20 years of accumulated teaching tools into a truck and made six trips to my new school.

As I moved in box after box, I was hit with that familiar fragrant smell of an old school—a combination of cleaning products, boys' bathrooms, and aging walls. I breathed in that wonderful scent and let out a sigh of relief because I was certain that I had come home.

While teaching in the previous district, I had been recognized for the Presidential Award for Excellence in Teaching Mathematics and Science, State Teacher of the Year, the Milken Educator Award, and National Board Certification. I wanted to leave all baggage behind so I asked my new principal not to share any of my background with staff. For as long as possible, I wanted to be just a teacher—nothing more, nothing less.

My new assignment was also fourth grade. In my former fourth grade, no one was below grade level, 10 students were identified as gifted, and one student was reading *The Yearling* independently. In my new fourth grade, no one was above grade level, one student was identified as gifted, and one student was reading *Brown Bear, Brown Bear* with assistance. When some specialists saw my class roster, they shuddered and offered sympathy and support. Despite their pessimism, I felt energized and optimistic.

On the first day of school, I discovered none of my fourth graders could identify a continent or a country because they did not understand the difference between the two. I took a deep breath, inhaling that familiar, fragrant old-school smell, and resolved to add more tricks to my teacher bag.

My present district requires that every teacher, within the first three years of employment, take a course called "Essential Elements of Instruction." I decided to enroll immediately. Several years before I had taken classes covering the same material so I did not expect to learn many new tricks. However, I soon discovered something more valuable—I could absorb and apply the content more efficiently and effectively. In addition, I signed up for workshops in science, oral reading, literacy frameworks, and discipline.

Several months into the year I found myself surveying the class during one of those rare, tranquil moments only an elementary teacher understands and appreciates. At about 10 a.m. our assignment was "silent read." A conduct-disordered and mildly mentally handicapped student was asleep again on pillows under my desk—probably another late night out and about, "visiting" with mom.

An autistic and moderately mentally handicapped child was coloring cats in the corner. One student, on too many meds for asthma and allergies, was already in "Australia" for his second cool-down. Another, who suffers from anxiety and ADHD, had his upper body under his desk with his shirt drawn tightly over his head. I could not see if he was reading (probably not).

A mildly mentally handicapped student was struggling to read *Frog and Toad*, while another student, with an IQ of 126 who could not read *Frog and Toad*, was pretending to read a Nintendo brochure. For now I wanted to savor the moment. Most students were engrossed in a book. I had no shortage of stories.

In June, when the books were put away, the shelves covered, and the last desk stacked, I stood alone in the classroom. I took a deep breath, again savoring the fragrant familiar smell of my new "old school." I heard the laughter of the children, saw the light of their learning, and felt the pulse of their lives. Not once this year did I find myself repeating the litany, "I can and I will, I can and I will." Instead, I knew I could and I would, because the niggling rash of discontent was gone. My spirit was salved and refreshed by the stories of my students. "I am a teacher and I would be none other."

Changing Students' Attitudes About Failure With One Word: Overload

JEFF McADOO

Lawrence, Kansas

Most educators will agree that the quickest, most efficient learning takes place at the *frustration level*, where students are struggling and the material to be learned is challenging. This applies to any learning, whether it is math, reading, or shooting basketballs. The problem is convincing students to be willing to work at the frustration level, because doing so guarantees experiencing failure.

To determine the potential strength of raw materials used in manufacturing or building trades, they are stress-tested until they break (fail). This is the only way to know their capabilities. For human beings to discover their individual capabilities on any given skill, they must push that skill to the point of failure. Only then can they know their limits and at what point they should be working for maximum improvement.

If our students are afraid to fail, how can they ever know their own capabilities? If they don't know their own capabilities, how can they know at what level they should be working for the most efficient use of their learning time? How can teachers know at what level their students should be working for the most efficient use of learning time if those students are not encouraged to work to the point of failure?

Through the use of the word "overload," students at Quail Run Elementary in Lawrence, Kansas, have become better risk takers and more willing to work at their individual frustration level. Several years ago I began teaching my K-6 students about overload by stating, "The only way to make a muscle stronger is to 'overload' it—to make it do more than it is used to doing." Once they understood this concept for muscle development, it was very simple to transfer it to skill development. "Whether it is doing jump-rope tricks, shooting baskets, reading, playing piano, or writing, the only way to get better is to do more than you are used to doing—to overload."

The next step was to build on the concept of overload, to sell them on the idea that failure was okay in a learning environment. Because some students think that physical education classes are a place to just have fun or play games, first I established "Why are we here?" (To learn.) Then I used the following questions and statements for discussion:

1. "How do you learn the fastest, by doing things that are easy or things that are difficult?" (Difficult.)

2. "If you are willing to try things that are difficult, what will probably happen?" (You will fail.)

3. "If you want to 'be the best you can be,' do you have to have the courage to fail?" (Yes.)

4. "It is okay to fail in a learning environment. In fact I expect you to do so many times each day." (Here is the time to differentiate between *learning time* and *performance*, or *testing time*. Failing during performance time or on a test is not desirable. But if you are willing to fail during the learning time, then, because you are overloading, you will do better during the test or performance.)

My students have heard from me many times that "I like it when you fail, because that means you are trying things that are difficult for you, and I love it when you learn from those failures!"

By introducing the overload concept in the gym, students can kinesthetically experience it and understand it before it is introduced in other classrooms. Then, classroom teachers can use the word "overload" to encourage students to extend themselves to be better risk takers, especially on nongraded assignments.

To an adult, this sounds simple and too easy—of course you have to try harder things to get better! But to a child, having the label "overload" helps them to use the concept at a conscious level, enhancing their knowledge of how to learn.

Embracing Change

JIM BROWN

Albany, New York

My very first job in teaching was fourth grade. I took over a class with five months left in the school year. By the end of that school year I can remember feeling like I could teach fourth grade until it was time to retire. When I found out that I would be teaching kindergarten the next year, I was petrified. Soon after the next school year began, however, I felt that I could teach kindergarten until it was time to retire.

At the end of that year I was told that I would be teaching sixth grade in the middle school. Not only would there be a new grade, but a new building, principal, and staff as well. I was mortified. At the end of that school year I was laid off due to budget cutbacks. Before the next school year began I obtained a job in a neighboring district. Although I was changing building and district, I was happy that I would still be teaching sixth grade.

The greatest lessons I learned from all that change was that change was good and that in order to survive I had to ask for help from as many people as I could. It is normal for people to fear the unknown. However, if we are not willing to make a change, we could be missing opportunities. I learned what I liked about teaching at different grade levels. There is more than one way to run a building, and I learned that first-hand—I didn't just read about it. I could see the pluses and minuses for myself and was able to verbalize them to others. I also met new friends and colleagues, which enabled me to network with more people.

Now when an opportunity for change does not present itself quickly enough, I seek it out. In education, there are many opportunities for change—sometimes whether you want it or not. There are new classes each year, new principals and colleagues to work with, new curricula to teach, and so on and so forth.

My most recent opportunity was the introduction of computers into the classroom. Rather than not using the computers because I did not know everything about them, I shared with the students that I was learning right along with them. If a student asked me a question about the computer that I could not answer, I first asked the rest of the class if they knew the answer. Most of the time one of the students did. If no one knew, we would look it up together. Although I am still not an expert, I have improved a tremendous amount. Recently a book (about using computers in the social studies classroom) that I coauthored was published.

When you find yourself facing something new, embrace it. The worst you can do is fail. Even in failure, you are learning. You have learned what does not work. If you know someone who is considering doing what you have failed at, you can give him or her your insight. That can be valuable information. You never know where new opportunities may take you.

You are more likely to regret having passed an opportunity wondering "what if" than having accepted an opportunity and failing at it.

Immersion to Inspiration

ERIKA REYNOLDS

Pascagoula, Mississippi

A t 3 a.m., after driving most of the night, my husband
and I pulled the mattresses from the back of the U-Haul
and threw them on the floor of our new apartment. We were
relocating from Florida where I had been teaching kindergarten, my first love. I took the fourth-grade job that I was
offered, but I was not thrilled.

After a few hours of sleep, I arrived at my new school as
the new kid on the block, nervous and excited about the challenges that were ahead. During the staff meeting, the first-
year principal, who had been sent to turn around this failing
school, announced that there was a kindergarten position
available due to the late retirement of a teacher.

I could hardly sit still. This would be perfect. All of my
teaching materials could be used—the ones that took up over
half of the U-Haul. Immediately after the meeting, I asked to
be moved to kindergarten since my experience and materials
were perfect for the position. It couldn't happen. I was then
shown a nice classroom with four walls. This wasn't mine. I
was taken to the gym. My fourth-grade classroom was here,
along with a special education class and the Parent Center.

We were divided only by three-foot folding walls. There
were only tables and chairs—no manipulatives, paper, or
supplies. I was disheartened, but knew I had to make the best
of it. I began the year with the fourth graders attempting to
involve them in learning. They did not know how to handle
the hands-on learning because it was new to them.

I became very frustrated and had no one in the building
to turn to. Things began to look up when the principal
announced in a staff meeting that grants would be available
through our central office using Eisenhower funds. I spoke up
to tell the staff about how easy it was to write a grant, which I

knew firsthand because I had received three while teaching in Florida.

At this point, the principal was thrilled to know that I could help her. This opened the lines of communication. Then, unexpectedly a month after school began, she had to open another first-grade class.

I became the Grade 1 teacher. I still stayed in the gym, but was much happier with the curriculum and the age of the students. The other teachers chose the students who I would receive. The principal stopped by to observe my classroom and saw the centers I was using to teach reading.

She came and told me to go observe the other classes. I did and saw children sitting in rows facing the blackboard and reciting. This was not how I believed children learned. However, I knew I couldn't go against the principal completely. Thus, I wrote two grants that required hands-on learning in math. I received both of them and therefore had the support of the district.

I was able to implement more hands-on learning through centers due to the implementation of the grants. I modified the instruction during reading to be more in line with the other classes and I was still able to work in the strategies I felt were most effective with my students.

HELPFUL TIPS

While I was in graduate school, the reading of professional literature changed the course of my teaching. I have kept my practices on the cutting edge because of this literature. I read constantly. I surround myself with other like-minded colleagues. While teaching second grade, I found a kindergarten teacher who shared the same passion. We could talk for hours about education and teaching strategies.

I was able to influence others by sharing my passion for professional reading. Due to the fact that we kept up with education, our principal allowed us and trusted us to step out and try something different. She knew we were doing what we felt was best for the children.

I am now teaching kindergarten at the elementary school I attended. I said I would never do that—never say never. I have been able to influence others again with the reading of professional literature. I have shared these books with my colleagues and at workshops I have given. If there is anything teachers can do to keep their practices fresh, it is to read professionally. There is a wealth of literature written by real teachers.

Finding someone to discuss this literature with is also very important. Even after 11 years in the classroom, I want to stay abreast of the trends in education. When new mandates come, I am able to take and utilize the parts that are necessary. However, I always put my own little twist on it.

Because I keep up with what's going on in the field, I am asked or I volunteer to be on curriculum committees. This gives me the opportunity to influence new mandates. I continue to write and receive grants. When there is something I find that will better my classroom or teaching strategies, I write a grant. I am not afraid to go to others and ask for help or funding.

Facing the Old and New

PETER RIFFLE

West Lawn, Pennsylvania

I began teaching in the late 1960s and have seen more educational changes than I care to remember. Every few years a pioneer in education comes out with a new learning theory. Frequently these concepts deal with reading, math, or a combination of the two. It seems like everyone perceives these new programs as the shining light that will inspire students to learn at an accelerated speed.

Each novel method guarantees to have "Bobby" reading on a college level before he leaves third grade. I vividly remember when the *new math* technique hit the educational airwaves. This was the only way math should be taught. It sure was a great plan: Bobby could recite countless mathematical theories, but couldn't add two plus two!

The teachers who seem to be most affected by these revolutionary educational proposals are the young professionals. Why? They lack the experience of the more seasoned veterans who have been around this block a few times. The older teachers have run the gauntlet and are more cautious with these trendy programs.

Inexperienced teachers must be prepared for numerous changes throughout their teaching careers. In order not to push the panic button, they must stay focused on what is of paramount importance—the kids. I strongly doubt if any of these highly touted new methods, forced upon you by your administrators, will cause irreversible harm to your students. I'm sure you will find both good and bad in these state-of-the-art programs. Take the positive characteristics and use them; modify or disregard the negative aspects.

Many years ago, when discussing the impending birth of my first son with the obstetrician, he told me something that I've never forgotten when dealing with new ideas. He said, "Don't be the first to throw out the old and don't be the first to embrace the new." This sums up my belief on innovative educational curricula.

In closing, I would like to say that for all of the new ideas yet to be published, the one common denominator that stays constant is a dedicated, enthusiastic, caring teacher. Truthfully, no matter how incredible this new venture might be, the ship never leaves the dock without the captain at the helm. The students will not positively respond to any instructional process unless they connect with the teacher. Children don't care about how much you know; they will only know how much you care.

Why Are We Here?

JEFF McADOO

Lawrence, Kansas

D
o your students really know why they are in school? Each subject area in the field of education has its own set of activities. But are the activities the end goal or just the tools with which to attain that goal? Maybe it is more important that the students know the difference between the tools and the goal. As teachers, we know we are all in the classroom to learn, but if we assume that the students understand this, we can be handicapping our students.

For example, what is the purpose of a literature class—just to read books or to learn about good writings and maybe even how they have affected the world? What is a chemistry class for—just to do cool experiments or to use those experiments to learn about the elements and how they can impact each other and us?

In physical education classes, do you just play games or do you learn how to use those games as tools to stay healthy? What is a building trades class for—to build a coffee table or to learn how to use the tools of the building industry?

Relevance motivates and if our students only know *how* to do the activities, but not *why*, then why should they care about the subject? Teachers need to make sure, and not assume, that students know that the answer to "Why are we here?" is "To learn!"

Since the elementary physical education classroom is usually a fun place, very often students think the main reason for being there is not to learn, but to have fun. Why should they think otherwise unless I change their minds? Each year at the beginning of the very first physical education session for every class except kindergarten, I give the students an informal test with one question, "Why are we here?" This question is written on a large piece of paper as follows:

Why are we here?

1. To have fun?

2. To get into shape?

3. To do sports?

4. To learn?

5. To win?

They are instructed to show me with their fingers the number of which answer is the most important reason we are in physical education class. We then discuss that, yes, we will have fun, but that is not the reason we are here. And, yes, we will work on getting into better shape, but that is not the reason we are here, and so on.

Once it is established that we are in physical education class to learn, it is very quick and simple, at any time, to refocus the group when they get overly competitive, too silly, or too serious with a simple question of "Why are we here?" followed by their response of "To learn!"

I have been amazed at the results of using this simple question. I teach eight class periods of elementary physical education every day. I use that question in probably seven of those eight classes each day and often more than once in a single class.

It *never fails* to make an impact, get the students' attention, and help me smoothly transition into the next part of the lesson. In worst-case scenarios, the students might moan the answer that they know I want, but even with a bad attitude, the question makes it simple to redirect the students as needed.

This may seem incredibly simple, and it is. But like a mission statement for any organization, it can very effectively get your people back on task.

Changes in
Curriculum and
Instruction

Education Issues and Trends

COLLEEN COOPER

Missoula, Montana

Pick up a newspaper or magazine or watch the nightly news, and you will read or hear about some issue that is related to education. School funding, achievement scores, class size, discipline techniques, and teacher salaries are just a few of the educational issues that I have seen in the media recently. However, I believe that one of the major public education issues of today is rarely reported on or even discussed: Our teachers are suffering from low self-esteem.

When we first begin teaching we are full of energy, creativity, and positive thoughts and filled with the belief that "I can do anything." As the demands of the job take over we often feel helpless and ineffective when tackling the situations that cause our children to come to school less than prepared to learn. We all too frequently give in to the idea that there are too many outside factors that are affecting our effectiveness as teachers. When teachers start thinking like this, they give away their power to make a difference in children's lives. In order to eliminate that type of thinking we must surrender our old ways of thinking.

Some see surrendering those thoughts as a sign of weakness or failure. I see it as a sign that we are strong, we are in control, and we have the power to overcome obstacles. Some strategies that we can use to regain our self-esteem are to first look at our own beliefs about ourselves.

Do I act, think, and talk like a professional? Second, is my belief sincere in that all students can succeed or do I lower my expectations for students with special needs? Do I seek training and resources when I find a need to effectively serve students with a variety of needs? Do I make time for planning and meeting with team members and specialists so that I may elicit their ideas?

When I feel anxiety or fear because of my perceptions about my inabilities, do I seek advice and knowledge from other educators? We must resolve to increase our esteem and take back the honor and respect that our profession deserves, one classroom at a time.

Making Less Into More

Cindy Albert

Caribou, Maine

One wonders how we can possibly add more to the existing curriculum of an already jam-packed school day. As it stands now, we barely have enough time within the school day or year to fit in everything that should be taught. Every time we turn around we are faced with yet another new mandate or program that must be added to the curriculum.

We, as teachers, continue to do as we are told: add this new program, fit in this extra unit, extend this learning concept, and so on. Rarely do we rid ourselves of something to make room for these new programs; therefore, we now have less time to teach previous skills and concepts well. Often, such new syllabi are added at the expense of other areas of instruction.

In 1996, the Maine Legislature passed a bill adopting Maine's Learning Results. It includes a second language component titled Modern and Classical Languages. The Maine State Department of Education's plan for implementation of the Learning Results requires that all graduates will demonstrate proficiency of the Learning Results by the year 2005.

Our school department subsequently decided to implement a Foreign Language in the Elementary School (FLES) program during the 1999-2000 school year. Our rationale for implementation was that it would enable us to meet upcoming mandates in all academic areas. Research indicates that the younger the children are when they begin learning a second language, the more likely they are to become proficient and retain the language.

There is also substantial evidence that indicates young children who receive daily second language instruction show improved overall academic abilities such as increased problem-solving skills, listening skills, communication skills, and creativity. Learning a second language develops a clearer understanding of the English language and greater sensitivity to structure, vocabulary, and syntax. Second language learners score statistically higher on standardized tests conducted in English and demonstrate greater intellectual flexibilities.

Where did we find the extra time within our school day to include such extensive, additional programming? Our school opted to take advantage of the benefits afforded by second language instruction to improve learning in the first language.

Additionally, we scheduled second language instruction within the literacy time block of the regular classroom, where communication skills are taught (understanding, speaking, reading, writing, language, spelling, etc.). While half of classroom A and half of classroom B are attending a daily 25-minute second language class, their respective other halves remain in the regular classroom with their own teacher.

There the students receive small group or individualized literacy instruction. The regular classroom teacher now has extra time with students and is better able to meet their individual instructional needs. The FLES program strives to develop listening and speaking fluency in a second language, improve appreciation of other cultures, and develop some proficiency in reading and writing a second language. All of this happens while they receive more individualized instruction from their classroom teacher.

The addition of the FLES program comes with little cost— a second language teacher salary and a few scheduling headaches! This is a small price to pay for all of the benefits. The students are the true beneficiaries, which supports the "children first" philosophy held by many educators.

The children learn a second language while receiving more personal lessons with their classroom teacher. Second language learners also reinforce and improve upon their academic skills in the first language. Parents are thrilled with the results thus far, and they along with the community are fully supportive of the addition of French instruction in the elementary schools.

Classroom teachers appreciate the invaluable individualized instructional time with their students. On the surface it may seem that implementing a new program must take something else away from the currently existing curriculum; however, *less* time can also mean *more* learning in the right conditions.

Thinking, Changing, Rearranging: A Compass Toward Affective Teaching

COLLEEN COOPER

Missoula, Montana

Early in my teaching career I read a poem and decided that my purpose for teaching would be "to build walls that empower children with self-esteem, knowledge, and a responsibility for self and others." Educational techniques, theories, classrooms, and students are in a constant state of change.

I realized that to be an effective teacher and deal with these changes I needed to focus on what all children need and require to thrive: to be touched affectively. I believe that children will not always remember what I have said but they will remember how I made them feel.

Throughout my varied teaching experiences as a regular and special educator, I have learned the importance of teaching the child as an individual as well as teaching content. I believe I facilitate the process of uniting children and their responsibility for learning with the guidance of family and a supportive school atmosphere. Teaching is an art. When we ask writers or actors or painters how they do what they do so well, we will often hear how they blend the techniques, methods, and skills of their trade with their own innate abilities to truly make a masterpiece.

My instructional techniques are eclectic. I believe that I have the knowledge of how to use the best instructional techniques in the many situations that happen in a classroom comprising various learning abilities. I have a wealth of methods and techniques available to me that I have learned from various educators. These are the tools of my trade.

Within my classroom I use direct teaching, peer teaching, cooperative learning, team teaching, collaborative teaching, station teaching, and self-teaching. The longer I teach, the more I realize the impact of not teaching content but of teaching children.

The true art of teaching comes when we influence children's attitudes and turn them on to helping and learning for themselves as well as others. In this rapidly changing world our young come to us in the school environment often with the belief that there are just too many factors in their lives that they cannot control and often those factors lead to their belief that they are not and never will be successful. It is my job to blend their academic success with the belief that they do have a choice every day regarding their attitude and outlook on life.

They cannot change their past or the fact that certain people will act certain ways, but they can change their future by the choices that they make today. They can change how they perceive the world and their attitude about events happening around them.

I believe that teaching is a partnership with the universe. We are shaping human character and determining destiny through the lives that we touch in our classroom daily.

Student-Centered Objectives: Solid Grounds in the Tides of Change

MaryEllen Daneels

West Chicago, Illinois

The world of education is in a constant state of change. My classroom today is much different than it was when I first started teaching. Today, I teach an interdisciplinary course, which allows me to collaborate with professionals from other disciplines. Each of my courses is supported by a Web page that informs both students and parents and facilitates student assignments.

I also use threaded technology to allow students to communicate with one another between classes on curriculum. I have developed and taught new courses in the school (community leadership and Latino studies) based on student interests and needs. Cooperative learning, problem-based learning, and writing across the curriculum are strategies that I use on a daily basis.

While all of these changes have helped me become a more effective teacher, I believe that there is one element that has anchored me in the ever-changing currents of education. This anchor is a commitment to student-centered objectives. I believe the identification and revision of these objectives is one of the most important elements of a resilient teacher.

Student-centered objectives provide a firm foundation upon which to build a successful classroom. Clear objectives allow me to analyze the latest innovations in technology, teaching strategies, evaluation, and the like to discern which will best help me meet the objectives that have been established for the course.

These objectives serve as a compass to guide my lesson plans. As a history teacher, I have 11 years more of content than I did when I started teaching and the same amount of time to do it in. How do I decide what to add? What do I cut? Objectives steer these important decisions.

My department chair and mentor has been a leader at our school in developing student-centered questions to guide our curriculum. For example, a traditional United States history course will have a unit titled "The Civil War." Everyone agrees that this is an important area of history to cover, but why?

Examining the Civil War through answering the question "When is revolution justified?" gives focus to content in a way that is meaningful to students and gives a basis for students to analyze the material and connect it to the past and the future.

It allows me as a teacher to let go of some material, such as the name of General Lee's horse, and focus on issues of civil rights, state's rights, federalism, and the like in the interest of helping students to answer the focus question.

The invention and revision of these mission statements for my curriculum and the assimilation of new information and strategies to better serve student needs has helped me thrive in the constantly evolving world of educational reform. Otherwise, I would drown in the tides of change, for I would have no means to navigate through these waters, no solid ground to stand on.

Note. To access the Web pages, which include focus questions, please see the department and curriculum Web pages on the Community High School District 94 Web site.

HELPFUL TIPS

Below are some teaching tips I have found useful over the years. I hope this proves helpful to you.

1. "Those who do not learn from history are condemned to repeat it."

Take time at the end of each day to reflect back on your lessons. What worked? What would you change? Keep notes in your plan book to this effect so next time you may need the lesson, you have an accurate record to build on.

2. Be humble; go to the experts.

Ask the experts in your community to help you with lesson planning or even to come in to be the guest teacher for the day. I have asked our art teacher to come in on occasion to share his knowledge to enrich my world history classes. Our local historical society has sent professionals in to teach students about the ways in which history is uncovered and examined through a primary source lab.

3. Need an idea? Go surfing.

Once upon a time, teachers would spend hundreds of dollars a year on lesson plan idea books, simulations, and the like. Today, you can find a lesson on just about anything on the Internet. Don't think of these lessons as the final word but a starting point that can inspire you and be modified.

    4. Make connections.

Our school has quite a few interdisciplinary courses. This has led teachers who are not part of interdisciplinary teams to make their own connections. American history teachers and American literature teachers are talking to each other and English teachers are teaching books that line up chronologically with the history being taught. For example, *The Scarlet Letter* is being taught at the same time the history classes are studying the early colonies. Teachers make an effort to show the relationships between the classes and the students have a richer experience for it.

Changes in Instruction: Change Is Not Always Easy

KRISTEN DEWITT

Kalamazoo, Michigan

My understanding of the goal of education is to create responsible citizens, independent thinkers, and lifelong learners who understand themselves and the world around them. Successful educators, therefore, have a responsibility to research, collaborate, and implement programs that will achieve this goal. They should be comfortable enough with themselves to accept change, yet skeptical enough to research its effectiveness.

    Whenever I am faced with the opportunity to help choose a new textbook series or develop a new area of the curriculum

I try to focus on one simple question: Is this best for kids? With this question in mind I made a decision three years ago which I believe will change the way I teach forever. Together with our supportive building principal, my two dedicated teaching partners and I implemented a third, fourth, and fifth grade multiage program in my district.

While this was not a mandated change, it required planning and acceptance just the same. Multiage education is not a new concept and has been implemented in many areas of the country for decades. In my district, however, it was new to all, confusing to many, and threatening to some. Like all new programs, our multiage program was met with a combination of support and dissension.

My two teaching partners and I spent a year researching the pros and cons of multiage teaching and convincing others in our district, as well as in our community, of its benefits for our students. The hard work and dedication paid off and my days of teaching in seclusion were over. Our multiage program, which was originally approved as a three-year pilot, was formally accepted as a permanent program in the district after its third successful year.

Teaching in a multiage setting has positively impacted my role as a successful teacher. As our program has grown and developed I've made many changes in my teaching strategies and classroom practices that I feel are best for kids. While all of these changes have helped me become more effective, the most powerful changes relate to collaboration with colleagues, involving the community, and self-reflection.

The biggest change and most beneficial aspect of multiage education for me is team teaching. If my teaching is going to be effective, collaborating with my partners is essential. We meet several times a day to plan lessons, discuss student concerns, and share the workload.

We also meet with upper elementary teachers in our building and teachers from other districts interested or involved in multiage education. This extra time and effort ensures better-prepared and more meaningful lessons for our students.

Working with the community and maintaining open communication is another change I've made. Inviting the community into our classroom and viewing it as an important resource was essential to the development of our program and is a part of its continued success.

We view the community as an extension of the classroom and, therefore, included its members in our original planning team. We continue inviting members of the community to enrich the curriculum and enhance student learning. Parent volunteers are also welcomed and involved in planning activities and working with students.

Reflection has allowed me to look at myself and make changes within. I find that I am now constantly assessing my own teaching and reflecting on my own practices. I ask my teaching partners to make observations during lessons and am appreciative of feedback they give.

I use the feedback to consider how I teach and the impact my teaching style has on my students. I have videotaped my teaching and studied it to gain insight into my interactions with my students. Through reflection, I am able to better understand my effectiveness as a teacher.

I believe that by being open-minded and willing to learn about multiage education, both my students and I have benefited. The implementation of our program has helped me as an educator to achieve my goal of creating responsible and independent lifelong learners.

By constantly asking if this is best for kids, we've developed a successful program that is being considered by other buildings in our district. The time, effort, and determination required to implement this program have been difficult at times, but the changes I've seen in my students and my teaching are well worth it.

HELPFUL TIPS

Cooper Elementary is a small, rural school with approximately 180 students and two each of half-day kindergarten, first, and second grades. We offer one Grades 3-5 multiage class as well as one each of third, fourth, and fifth grades. Near the end of second grade, parents are encouraged to request that their child be placed in either the traditional or the multiage program. We do, however, balance the classes according to age, gender, ability, and behavior differences and have the power to override a request.

Students are strongly urged to remain in either program for the entire three years, although we have had minimal movement of students from one program to the other for a variety of reasons. I'd been teaching for Plainwell Community Schools for two years when our building principal approached the staff regarding innovative programs.

He encouraged us to research any program we thought interesting and let him know how he could support us. Several teachers and I were familiar with multiage education and jumped at the chance to learn about it. We formed a strategic planning group, visited multiage programs, and spoke with Department of Education leaders and university professors familiar with it.

One year later, three of us decided it was definitely worth trying and began to approach the Board. After several board meetings, parent gatherings, and union meetings, we were approved. We began construction to join three classrooms, attended various staff development workshops, and began planning.

We worked with our curriculum director to rearrange our three-year curriculum into thematic units that could be used on a three-year rotating basis. We also rewrote our report cards to accommodate our themes.

The following year we began (as a three-year pilot program) and the Board hired an independent research group to conduct a long-term study comparing student achievement of our students and the traditional third, fourth, and fifth grade classrooms. The group presented this spring with excellent findings that supported our research. Our students were equally or more successful than their counterparts. These findings caused the Board to approve our program on a permanent basis and stimulated multiage interest in teachers and administrators in other buildings.

Standards-Based Instruction

MICHELLE MASH

Wilmington, Delaware

When I began my teaching career 12 years ago I did not begin the year with furniture (tables and chairs), manipulatives, or literature. I was hired due to an unexpected increase in enrollment. What I did have was a great deal of enthusiasm and an overabundance of workbooks.

I began using what I had—the many workbooks—and threw in my own creative ideas as much as possible. That year and the many years that followed in different districts provided several teacher's guides to the various curricular areas but the guidance and direction was limited. Different schools within the same district were teaching different content. The continuity and consistency for educators was missing.

Prior to state and district standards many teachers were choosing their favorite topic and integrating content into themes such as bears or dinosaurs. I struggled with this as an educator when I realized that if a child had certain teachers for Grades K-3, then the child would be studying the same topics each year. Most of the teachers used the same resources and went to the same workshops which we incorporated into our prior year's experience. My struggle came when I heard children say, "We did this last year."

There was so much to teach. I felt stuck and limited. Fortunately, I can honestly say that, with the Red Clay Consolidated School District standards and the Delaware State Standards and performance indicators, my teaching looks vastly different today.

Currently, I teach in a school community that dedicates itself to nurturing and educating all children in a way that values their individual differences and builds on each child's strengths. The district has embraced the State's standards, which drives my developmentally appropriate program.

The state of Delaware has worked for many years to provide each teacher with a teacher's desk reference. This large notebook contains standards that are developmentally appropriate and child centered. These standards are divided by grade and by content area. By implementing the standards-based instruction the goal is to improve student achievement and provide a common reference point to ensure that everyone has the same goals and expectations.

At first, the document seemed a bit overwhelming in size and number of goals. I was thrilled to have direction and expectations for the content I needed to cover in a year, but the next step was to decide how to apply the standards to my curriculum. The district inserviced the staff on how to use our desk references. Now I needed to find a way to easily implement them and to make them functional in the classroom.

One colleague made a chart with all the standards across the top and the children's names along the side. Then she would mark when the standard was introduced and when each child had mastered that standard. I have tried this approach for two years and it has gotten easier each time, but I still need to continue my efforts in managing this system.

Once the standards truly started to drive my instruction I did a lot of reflecting and asked myself why I used this method of instruction. I discontinued some things that I had done for many years because I could not validate their purpose. One other way I hold myself accountable is to write what standards I will be introducing or revisiting each month in my newsletter.

This has provided my administrators and parents with the content, curriculum, and specific standards I will address each month. Making this commitment has made me reflect on the previous month and helps me account for my teaching. Because of this I am much more focused and aware of the curriculum.

My pacing has been better because I am constantly reflecting, reteaching, and introducing standards. Because the standards are listed, the parents are more aware of what is going on in the classroom without physically being there. This allows the lines of communication to be open among all parties—the parents, children, and myself. Parents can ask their child probing questions about the curriculum, introduced with knowledge of the standards mentioned in the newsletter.

I feel more directed and focused with the standards-based instruction. Because I am more effective and hold myself accountable the children are learning more. Personally and professionally, this has been an effective practice and has helped me to be a better teacher, which is a goal I strive to achieve every day!

Successfully Teaching a High-Poverty Student Population

KIMBERLY ALLEN

Glendale, Arizona

With the constant change in education, one thing remains the same: children need consistency, constant encouragement, and positive role models. Four years ago, when I was an eighth grade math and science teacher, it was important that I employed teaching strategies that were solid, basic, and consistent with a high-poverty, itinerant population. My students couldn't waste their precious learning time on the latest fad in education. It was important that I be the constant in their life of variables.

For most of our student population, the basics of quality teachers, enough textbooks, basic supplies, or even having a place to do homework are not a part of their surroundings and therefore influence a student's ability to learn. Therefore, it became critical for me to provide learning opportunities that employ solid, basic teaching techniques that sequentially move students along a continuum to master the curriculum.

Using my prior 10 years of special education teaching experience, I sought to take the crucial elements of individualizing and apply those elements to the class as a whole. This approach offered a variety of levels of difficulty, a variety of activities, a team effort, cooperation, and a commitment of high expectations. This approach also stopped the cycle of low expectations and mediocrity. As students were challenged to rise above the academic standards of the past and break the cycle of low expectation and mediocrity, they had an opportunity to see and believe in themselves as high achievers in either school or life.

In designing both my math and my science curricula, the following occurred.

Integrated Curriculum. Through the implementation of block scheduling, I was able to completely integrate both curricula. This integration made the learning more applicable and real to the students because most activities are complex and interrelated anyway. I was also very fortunate to extend this integration with the language arts and social studies teacher next door to my classroom so that total integration of a theme could be explored.

Hands-On Procedures. Most anything that can be learned can be learned hands-on. Block scheduling also allowed for many hands-on activities to take place because it allowed for plenty of time for an activity to be completed and thoroughly investigated. My students realized that I could teach a topic by lecture and notetaking or they could be actively involved from beginning to end.

Result-Oriented Activities. As motivating as it was for students to get involved with an activity, it was even more rewarding when it culminated in a finished project. One of our most creative and engaging productions was the creation of a room-size space station called the Mirage 2000. Students were involved in all aspects of creating a walk-through exhibit that allowed students in Grades 4-8 to experience what life might be like in space.

Even though I didn't live in the community, I brought my own children to the school. I believe this sent a message to not only the students but also their parents about my commitment to the quality of education I wanted and continue to strive toward for *all* children.

Ultimately I believe my passion for children and teaching made my everyday classroom practices interesting and vibrant to my students. My students knew that I loved working with them and wanted to be there with them.

HELPFUL TIPS

Accepting All Students. Our job is to teach the kids parents send us. Not the ones we used to have and not the ones we would like to have, but the ones we have now—*all* of them.

Failure Should Never Be an Option. Always give the test again and always be fair.

Student Achievement Is up to the Teacher. Student achievement equals teacher effectiveness. If we teach better, they learn better. If we teach more, they learn more. If we teach them all, they all learn.

Closing the Achievement Gap. The kids at the bottom cannot be expected to change or improve their achievement unless their teachers change and improve their teaching.

Changes in Curriculum and Instruction

CARMELLA ETTARO

West Hills, California

Important years, turning points—1988, a summer math institute at Princeton, and 1989, a national math conference—until then I had never gone to math workshops out of state. For years I heard the same speakers and presentations at local meetings, at times conducting sessions myself.

At Princeton, the caliber of lecturers was outstanding. Working with other teachers on projects and having my ideas validated gave me tremendous confidence that still sustains me today. The National Math Conference was being held in Orlando. My first thought was Disney World! So with a colleague we went the weekend before and enjoyed the park.

What came afterward has influenced and changed my philosophy about curriculum forever. The issue was integrated versus traditional curriculum in mathematics. After carrying back texts and materials on the plane, numerous meetings and inservices resulted in the changeover within five years to a completely integrated sequence. When integrated programs are implemented correctly, they work. At my school, more students, especially girls, are taking four good years of mathematics.

The math wall hit by students was proofs in geometry in the second year of high school math. The wall is still there but now it is in the third year. Keeping students longer in the college prep sequence has been a measure of success I am proud of. The redesigning of math curriculum is very rewarding and a challenge that I look forward to.

It wasn't very long until the backlash started. It takes teachers longer to plan lessons and come up with innovative ways to teach and test in this curriculum. The premise is to connect the mathematics with applications to what students know and are interested in. There is little "drill and kill" type exercises. I can't remember the last time a student asked, "When are we ever going to use this?"

Parents and tutors couldn't help their child since it didn't look like what they had—more thinking and understanding are involved. The integrated program we adopted simply shifted the topics to different years, spread out the geometry, and de-emphasized some concepts such as factoring. After extensive inservice, many teachers in other schools decided it was too much work.

Soon the state officials began listening to traditionalists and some professors who suddenly received students into their classes who could think and use visual presentations but not factor 50 problems. By 2000, the math wars had turned bloody.

State money is now being tied to buying traditional books. Abstract algebra out of context is the only type that can be taught, no technology use on tests, and so on. Positive achievements such as rising test scores, increased senior math class enrollments, and the school ranking in the top 5% are ignored.

The adoption cycle began again in 2001. At first I felt as if I were standing at the bottom of a mountain that I had already climbed and conquered. The question I faced was, "Do I take the first step up and begin the fight again?" I am tired. It's been 30 years of trying to find the best strategies and curriculum to teach the students.

And now once again, mathematics education is being dictated by outside forces that have never seen the reality of the classroom of today or kept current as to the mathematics needed by the students of tomorrow. When I hear that attaining calculus is the only measure of success, I shudder at the ignorance of ignoring the need for statistics and computers. Throughout the years I have learned that the support from colleagues is crucial to survival in the classroom.

Our department office is quite small and is shared by 16 teachers. Due to the shortage of rooms, we also share classrooms. We have become a cohesive group. To help make the decision as to whether I fight for our programs, there was no hesitation in my convening the department members and asking what they felt and wanted me to do. Without their support and vote of confidence I would not have taken that first step. Teachers can no longer work in isolation. The support I received that day has put me back into battle. Win or lose, I will survive because of that support. It is more discouraging this time, as there are more people in decision-making roles that do not teach or know the students of today.

Teachers can no longer work in a vacuum. They need to know that what they think and do is valid to their peers. It is crucial that teachers attend conferences and workshops to hear what is going on in the rest of the country and world. Isolation has become the demoralizing factor that stifles good teachers and teaching. My department and I cope by connecting and seeing what others outside our state are doing.

A department should be made up of a team of teachers all working toward the common goal of providing four good years of mathematics. The calculus teacher may receive the credit for a successful class, but it is the vertical team effort of the teachers who prepared those students prior to this course that is important.

One of my department members, in accepting an award, once said to me that what I do the best for the department is to take good teachers and make them better, both professionally and mathematically, by continuing to encourage them to be lifelong learners themselves. What my department does not realize is how much I depend on them to cope with the everyday challenges and decisions I must make.

No longer a person who simply orders supplies and sits passively on committees, today's effective department chair needs to be involved in the curriculum process and in turn mentor the teachers by giving them support and encouragement to try new technologies, strategies, and innovative lessons.

Articulation among colleagues must be ongoing. I feel I need to model this to the department and to delegate as soon as possible lead teacher roles to others. The concept of lead teachers is something I started many years ago as a way to keep and pass on lessons from teacher to teacher as new teachers are given existing courses. Too often I've seen good courses cease to exist because they are teacher dependent.

I strongly believe teachers need to develop their own style and at the same time incorporate and learn from others who have taught the course. I won the State Farm Good Neighbor Award for developing an innovative unit with an assessment component. As lead teacher for analysis, I taught the others the unit and through the years it has grown and changed but is still done by all analysis teachers.

New teachers need to connect with the department and feel that they too can contribute. I expect anyone I hire to be a risk taker. A second-year teacher just completed a four-month car dealer simulation unit by having students learn all the jobs of a dealership and then bring the new cars on campus and have other classes participate by role playing.

He was so nervous that his heart was noticeably pounding. He told me he did not want to fail. I told him he would only fail if he did not try to reach these kids by doing something different. He had already succeeded in my eyes for daring to tackle this huge undertaking. It doesn't stop with new teachers. Each March 14th (Pi Day), we have a schoolwide celebration of mathematics. This includes a day of self-inservice to learn our new software acquisitions and equipment.

Our district motto is "High Expectations = High Achievement"; this coupled with the school's motto, "The Pride Is Inside," is what I expect and encourage in my department. No major change in curriculum can be successful without the teacher. What goes on in the classroom is the most important trigger for change. I continually discuss changes and what I expect to accompany them. I encourage conference attendance at least every other year.

I have learned to find the funds to send teachers and to buy the resources they need to make their classrooms better. I look for everyone to try one new thing a year. As students change, so do the strategies needed to reach them. I am continually being teased that I will have a career in charity fundraising after I retire.

Decision making is shared and commonplace. Seniority is not a factor in assigning classes. Matching up of personalities with the types of classes and interests makes for a more successful program. I have a mother figure teaching the ninth grade honors class to love geometry and help them discover geometry is everywhere around us. She helps the kids make it through this difficult year. My former student teacher is the AP calculus teacher because he knows the technology needed to help them pass the exam.

Everyone needs a mentor for support. My first year of teaching was almost my last. The support of three strong women taught me a valuable lesson. A teacher in the classroom does know what students need. Now 30 years later, I apply this to my department by empowering the teachers to be involved in the curriculum process and to work as a team to bring out the best in themselves and their students.

Each Christmas I have a tea and invite those same three women and others who have given me support, along with the women teachers in the department. It is to thank the first group and to provide a model for the others to carry on the idea of support needed by teachers in education.

As John Donne said, "No man is an island, entire of itself, every man is a piece of the continent, a part of the main . . . " and so is the department to me. Without their support, humor, and openness to my ideas, I would not be able to be as creative in my own classroom, to share my excitement for some wonderful new idea for a lesson, or to continue my enthusiasm for teaching.

More Changes in Curriculum and Instruction

LLOYD BARBER

Evanston, Illinois

Changes in curriculum and instruction can often be more difficult for parents than for children. Young children especially are great risk takers and are very willing to attempt new tasks without hesitation. Adults, however, are much more cautious and find change unsettling.

In my elementary teaching career, I have taught all grades from kindergarten through Grade 5 and have always included a program that I designed titled "Spend a Day With Your Child." This program invites parents and guardians to spend at least one day each year in the classroom with their child. The adults have the opportunity to see exactly what their child is doing in a classroom setting, both academically and socially.

Introduction of a new curriculum is more easily facilitated when the parent or guardian sees firsthand what is happening in the classroom environment. Many of the questions (and sometimes fears) of a new curriculum are answered.

Another component that assists both in the introduction of a new curriculum and in maintaining a positive rapport with parents can easily be facilitated by hosting "Open Reading Day" three or four times during the year. Students and parents and guardians are invited into the classroom for the morning to read. Doors are closed, computers are turned off, phones are disconnected, and everybody reads. More than 75% of the parents of students in my class attend these sessions.

Children bring blankets, pillows, small stuffed animals, and so on as well as books for pleasure reading. Adults bring their work from the office, papers to write, or books for pleasure reading. Again, the parents and guardians have the opportunity to see their children in a positive educational experience.

New curriculum, new mandates, and new administrations should be seen as positive moves; after all, change is good!

Mainstreaming of New Populations

Karen Quillen

Sumner, Washington

The main type of mainstreaming has been and always will be those students with special needs. I feel as a teacher that it is my obligation to stay as current as possible on all aspects of teaching. Therefore when legislation first came to the forefront concerning mainstreaming I immediately took a workshop on exactly what this was and what it would mean to me.

That was in 1978; however, true mainstreaming did not actually take place in our district or surrounding districts until 1998, 20 years after my first exposure to it. In the past 20 years, I have attempted to stay current through attendance at conferences and development on task forces, and most recently as chairperson of an inclusion project.

One way to keep my classroom practice vibrant is to be the initiator of the change. Such is the case in our high school inclusion project. In addition, I try not to attempt too many tasks, which always results in less effective teaching. Therefore, if you embrace change rather than fight it, everyone becomes a winner.

First and foremost in my classroom is the education of all of my students. I am willing to change or implement change if that change will enhance or further educate my students. I have always felt that special needs students deserve the opportunity to be included in the regular educational setting, and finally the government agrees.

However, the process used to include all students is up for debate. Some teachers rebel against inclusion because it is more difficult to include all levels and behaviors in one classroom setting. Therefore, I feel that to initiate change or influence change, one must be an example to one's peers, which is what I try to do.

I continue to hold high standards in my classroom, but I am willing to recognize that curriculum modification may need to take place in order to educate all of my students. In addition, in order to influence change it is important to be involved in the decision-making facets of the school. For example, I am involved as a union negotiator for our new teacher contract this year.

I also have been a member of our leadership program through positions as math department chair, curriculum committee member, textbook adoption committee member, and master schedule committee member and through being on other less-prominent committees. In each of these committees, inclusion will have an impact, and by being in the forefront, I will help to mold change rather than simply initiate someone else's idea of what the changes to inclusion should look like.

Therefore, my number one practice or strategy to change in my classroom is to embrace it, not fight it. By being involved in the change process, it becomes easier to implement the changes. Stay flexible and recognize that changes that are not worthy of acceptance will surely fall by the wayside, given time. One can use change to improve teaching rather than try to fight change and end up with a state curriculum where everyone loses, especially students.

Putting Education to the Test

Introduction of New Tests and High-Stakes Tests

CARYN SMITH LONG

Charlotte, North Carolina

One of the opportunities that I had when I received the Presidential Award for Excellence in Math and Science Teaching this year was to attend a Congressional breakfast in which the Congressional representative for math and science teaching spoke.

During this session, we had the opportunity to line up and ask this representative questions or make statements on behalf of our state. I stood in line to share this comment on behalf of North Carolina's teachers: "President George W. Bush is looking at our state, North Carolina, as a leader in the field of accountability. I'm here to ask you to tell President

Bush to look somewhere else." Unfortunately, the congressman had to leave before I got to the microphone!

The introduction of high-stakes testing has done a lot of damage in this state. It was established in our statehouse by business leaders whose answer to everything is "produce some numbers." In the education field, the only numbers that can be produced are through standardized test scores. So, we have now reduced an entire year of education down to three days of testing in two limited subjects: math and reading.

The outcome of a test can be affected by the child's mood on those mornings, by events happening in the child's personal life, or by the overall health of the child. Now our state says that what a child does during the year doesn't really account for much. Only if students achieve a three or four rating on their tests will they pass their grade.

What happens to the child who has test anxiety and has made straight A's and B's during the year? The child retakes the test. If the child still doesn't pass, he or she goes to summer school. If the student doesn't pass again, he or she fails the grade.

The polar opposite of this case is the child who played around all year, did not do homework, failed in-class assignments, and still passes the standardized tests. The child passes the grade and has received the message that he or she only has to pass the test at the end of the year and does not have to follow through on daily work.

As for the teachers, principals, and superintendents, the message they have received during this age of high-stakes testing is that only reading and math count. We have switched from integrating curriculum, and making it meaningful, to isolating reading for two hours daily and mathematics for one hour daily. And what about science and social studies? Combine the time for these two subjects and alternate the days in which we teach them.

Math and literacy are not to be disturbed. If we have special programs (such as DARE or guest speakers), they are only to be done during social studies and science. In other words, social studies and science no longer count.

In a recent poll, a bipartisan group was asked, "What are the threats to our national security?" The number one threat was a nuclear strike to a major city. Second was the lack of good science teaching in our schools. With concern at such a high level, why are we isolating our subjects and de-emphasizing science?

Learning is meaningful to children only when it is made relevant to their world. This is a major cornerstone in the discovery method of instruction, which falls under the constructivist theory. Integrating subjects is by the far the best method in which to prepare students for their tests. By making the learning relevant, students are more likely to retain the information presented and apply it to a variety of situations. This enhances problem-solving skills.

In studies done in the El Centro School District in California, students' standardized test scores had risen 20 points over a three-year period through integration of the subjects using science as the tool for integration. This is an astonishing rate.

As part of the North Carolina Leadership Institute, it is my position that we retrain teachers, administrators, and superintendents about methods of integration using science as the tool to teach all other subjects. This has two benefits. First, by tying in all of the subjects with a common thread, students can properly scaffold their learning and build on previous knowledge.

Second, it opens up all subject areas to all students and provides all students with an opportunity to find their strength. Any educator who is familiar with Howard Gardner's multiple intelligences knows that individual students learn in a variety of ways.

One of the greatest detriments with high-stakes testing is the fact that social studies, science, and the arts are all cut out of an educational program for the sake of test preparation. Through integration, students can be exposed to all areas of study and individual talents can be developed.

New Mandates for Testing

AVALYN BALLIET

Irving, Texas

The state of Texas, like the rest of the country, is in love with the standardized test. We call it the TAAS or Texas Assessment of Academic Skills. We have lived with TAAS since the early 1990s and will have an updated version called TAAS II, or Son of TAAS as we lovingly refer to it, in 2003.

Beginning in 2002, the social studies portion of the TAAS test will be calculated in each school's report, the report card or accountability factor by which a school is rated exemplary, recognized, acceptable, or unacceptable. My school district and my history department are taking steps to prepare for this new mandate.

First, we are following in the footsteps of other disciplines by requesting help from them. We will attempt more cross-curriculum avenues by continuing to integrate reading skills into history classes and increase history content in the materials for reading classes. We already have a very successful Reading Across the Disciplines (RAD) program that practices main idea, inference, generalization, fact versus opinion, good listening behaviors, note taking, and previewing skills. It works very well in our middle school concept and teaming situation.

Now the challenge is to increase the historical literature (fact, fiction, children's picture books, young adult chapter books) in the reading program as it will correlate to the curriculum. Hopefully this approach will improve social studies scores as well as it has improved student achievement on the reading portion of TAAS.

Second, I have developed and implemented on my team a focus on test-taking skills. After my first two years of teaching, I recognized that my students did not know how to take a test. So I identified the thinking process commonly used to take a test: read, clues, eliminate, choose.

This may seem simple and be overlooked as innate to all students, but that premise is incorrect. My students have to be taught to read the entire question and decide if the question is something I have to know (a *brain* question) or something that the test will show me and I must find (a *book* question). Then they can look in the question, answer choices, passage, or prompt for clues to help them figure out the answer.

Elimination is the next key step to reducing the probability of getting an answer wrong, and after narrowing it down to two choices, correctly choosing the right answer. It is this process of logically thinking through a posed question that my students lack as much as vocabulary, content, or schema.

Last, I try to be adaptable by staying abreast of changing mandates and by using flexible strategies. I stay involved and read about current legislation. I write my government officials and speak up for the English as a Second Language and socio-economically disadvantaged kids. Who else will? I try to use proven strategies of cooperative learning, games, and drills, and write tests that are similar in format to the TAAS. By using benchmarking tests, I can identify those students who are deficient in skills and those who are close but need a little extra individualized help. Then we tutor those students in the spring and build up their confidence as TAAS approaches.

The biggest part of mastering any new mandate is to be flexible, adaptable, and willing to try new things in order to increase student achievement—whether that be for a standardized test or simply to equip them for the real world.

A High-Stakes Test

Sharon Jeffery

Plymouth, Massachusetts

In 1993, Massachusetts set out to reform education in the Commonwealth. This change began with writing standards for each subject within grade ranges. After a five-year period of drafts and revisions these standards were made the law for teachers. I often wondered how the state would ever know who was teaching to the standards and who wasn't. Who would be checking out every classroom?

I wasn't left wondering too long! Rumors flew of a state test which would verify that all the subjects were being taught as expected. Then the rumors were confirmed. The state department of education hired a company to write their Massachusetts Comprehensive Assessment System (MCAS), which would be given to every fourth, eighth, and tenth grader in the state. The worst part was that the tenth graders would eventually have to pass the exam in order to receive a high school diploma. We now had a high-stakes MCAS exam.

This sounded doom and gloom all over the place. Teachers revolted over the restrictions this put on their teaching. No more fun topics or diversions—now it would be *teach to the test* (as though that were the ultimate teacher sin). Threats flew of lost jobs, closed schools, and dismissed administrators. But what really happened? Teachers began teaching the state frameworks because administrators were watching closely.

I still had misgivings about this MCAS exam and just what it could prove or disprove. I applied and was accepted on the department of education's Science and Technology Writing Team. I saw the process firsthand and realized there were abundant checks and balances in the writing process, but vast disagreement over interpreting the standards and just exactly what students should know at any given grade level.

Administrating the MCAS fairly in every school took a plethora of rules and regulations. Some schools followed them closely, some adhered loosely, and some ignored them. The first results showed flaws in the scoring and that money seemed to play the largest part in a school system's success.

We watched the department of education backtrack on itself, change the passing score, and change writing companies. I saw students who had repeated eighth grade get all proficient scores and students who were consistently on the honor roll receive failing scores. This seemed odd to me—odd, but easily explained. These tests can't tell you much about a child's true ability as a student or a learner.

This revelation freed me from the fear of student failure. I can't make a child take this test seriously. I can't even force a student to answer the questions. I can't guarantee that I've covered every one of the minute details of a standard on which they could possibly ask a question. So what should I do?

I make sure my students can write a cohesive, factual essay. I regularly give my students open response questions so they are familiar with them. I go out of my way to force my students to think and praise them when they actually do it! I spend time telling kids daily, "You are smart!" Finally, I celebrate the two weeks it takes to administer the MCAS to my eighth graders by lightening the workload in class and using the time in class to encourage them to review what they know.

Changes in Funding, Class Size, School Populations, and More

Funding Issues

PERCY HILL

Andover, New Hampshire

When I began my teaching career in 1972, I was sure that I would set the world on fire with new ideas, innovative programs, and creative approaches to education. Still very wet behind the ears, I jumped into the vast sea of an ever-changing tide of educational reforms, funding issues, equal access to all curriculum, and major changes in the way communities viewed our education systems. I found myself in a whirlpool of educators truly wanting change that would honestly address the needs of students. I felt like a kid in a candy store with a pocket overflowing with money!

Creative and innovative programs were popping up everywhere. Children were finally being identified with specific learning needs and school communities were willing to fight for enhancement of educational opportunities that would look at the whole child. Many tremendous educational reforms were set in place that would address very specific needs of children: all children would receive an equal and relevant education.

I often wonder what the turning point was that made America look at the need for change in education. Perhaps it was the fear of being left in the dust by other world powers in technology and research, or maybe it was just the question "Why can't Johnny read?"

Regardless, funds flowed into our educational systems from federal and private sources like sand through a sieve to enrich the lives of children. Funds were made available to educate the gifted and talented child, educate children with learning disabilities, and establish experiential-based education, and a new appreciation for the arts became viable within our schools. Many communities expressed a new willingness to pay more for quality education for their children.

So, where have we evolved to and where are we going? I ask myself these questions every day and marvel at just how resourceful we all have become. The needs of a child are second to none. Each child does have the right to receive a quality education and nothing may stand in the way of enriching the life of each child, a huge responsibility that we take very seriously.

Funding for education programs has always been in question, and many facets of school life have changed considerably since 1972. Small communities in New Hampshire simply cannot afford to continually raise property taxes, and the more wealthy communities tend to have better schools. New Hampshire does not have an income tax or other sources of funding for education except for federal grants and money from the private sector.

Public school funding takes the largest chunk of taxpayers' money and the pocketbooks of the public have felt the ultimate squeeze. Families of lower- to low-middle income and the elderly on fixed incomes are affected the most by tax increases. Many towns throughout New Hampshire have cut budgets and have taken measures to assure the public that everything is being done to keep taxes (school spending) down.

Our town of Andover, New Hampshire, is not much different from other small, rural communities. We feel the economic crunch just like everyone else. Our K-8 public school of 261 students offers an excellent education for each child; we are very serious about addressing the needs of students individually and collectively.

My colleagues and administration are dedicated professionals who give of themselves well beyond the call of duty. Why? Andover professionals are living and breathing a true, self-fulfilling prophecy: Believe in and share a common mission for student achievement and make it happen.

Twenty years ago, I recognized that the children of Andover were deprived of cultural and social experiences. The lack of diversity and cultural difference was quite apparent in the (almost) all-Caucasian suburb in the middle of nowhere. Many children felt that a 45-mile trip to Manchester, New Hampshire, or a two-hour ride to Boston, Massachusetts, was the same as leaving the country! Proctor Academy (a fantastic private high school in town) was the only connection that most of the community had to cultural and social diversity. Many of the children and community thought of Proctor as a different world within our town and stayed away.

I had a vision for the children of Andover to help break the cycle of small town isolation. In 1984, I began developing programs that would take students away from their comfortable, familiar school setting and would go far beyond a field trip to the zoo. Children would experience nature through hiking, camping, and canoe and kayak trips and begin enriching their lives through esteem programs.

I arranged for volunteer assistance and borrowed as much equipment as necessary to make the programs happen.

I vowed that each program would not cost the school district any money and hence would be a zero expense to the community. When a program involved a fee (such as challenge or ropes course costs or transportation expenses) I asked the children to help with fund-raising events that would give something back to the community. Residents of Andover began to witness students taking responsibility for their education and displaying commitment and dedication beyond their wildest dreams: children making an investment in their future.

All that is only the tip of the iceberg. The more that I became engaged in a whole new dimension of student achievement, the more they (and I) wanted. I began looking more and more out of the box to truly meet the needs of Andover children. I happened upon one of the most amazing integrative education endeavors that sent me into a whirlwind of possibilities: learning through travel . . . children performing on unicycles.

The Andover One Wheelers Precision Unicycle Team was born in 1990. I began teaching children the skill of riding unicycles after school. My mission was to offer a K-8 free-of-charge program that would engage children in learning through commitment and dedication and would not cost the taxpayers any money.

The response for the program was overwhelming, and children from all grade levels came out to try the unicycle. I obtained five unicycles from donations (and my private stock), offered the program to anyone who wanted to learn, and the fun began. Within a very short period of time, over one third of the school population was riding unicycles! The new team of anxious, dedicated children performed at many local parades and New Hampshire Old Home Day events.

After only one year, the One Wheelers were invited to perform in the famous Macy's Thanksgiving Day Parade in New York City! We raised over $15,000 to make the adventure happen and the children gained national television and newspaper recognition. The children performed to an audience of millions and believe that Andover was put on the map because of them.

Since 1990, hundreds of children from Andover have gone through the program and have experienced learning through travel. The young ambassadors from New Hampshire have visited the Amish in Pennsylvania, toured our nation's capital, listened and watched in awe of the magnificence of Niagara Falls, and marveled at the mere sight of the Grand Canyon. The children from Andover have performed in over a dozen states and in Canada and have brought back journals and stories of their experiences to share with our school and community.

Is this free-of-charge education program expensive? You bet! The ballpark funds to operate the program have been nearly $200,000 over the past 11 years. Funds have come from traditional fund-raisers such as bake sales, car washes, and community dinners.

But countless numbers of private individuals and businesses have been very generous to help support the tremendous endeavor. All that was needed was to show something really working to enhance the lives of children, and ask. All of the people who work in the program work for the program and accept no money for their efforts. This program has become the baby of our community and everyone anxiously awaits the children's next adventure.

I believe that programs exist throughout the United States that require funding beyond school budgets and I know that there are other people out there who will not allow money to get in the way of educating children.

Changes in Class Size and Teaching Load

CLAUDE ARCHER

Miami, Florida

As funding for education continues to lag behind population growth in many areas, teachers find themselves with an increasing number of students in their classrooms. This trend has been particularly evident in exceptional student education classrooms where class sizes grow to the bursting point before additional staff allocations are made.

One year I found myself with a student load of 52 students diagnosed as specific learning disabled, emotionally handicapped, and mentally handicapped in a resource room while I waited for the district to provide assistance in the form of a second teacher.

I used several survival strategies during that year and have continued to use them daily, particularly when I find my class size growing. Two of the most effective tools for me were learning centers and effective time management.

Learning centers require more planning than most instructional activities and students must be able to work at the centers independently. Center activities should match individual student learning goals, be challenging and engaging, and allow students to assess their own learning. They should also provide the teacher with information about students' strengths and weaknesses as well as their progress.

Learning centers allowed me to work with smaller groups of students on specific skills and goals while the other students rotated among the centers during a specified period of time each day. Before beginning with centers, I always showed the entire class what the activities were and how they would be used.

I would also select an expert from the class and train that student to answer all questions about one center so that the classmates could refer to him or her. Learning centers can be commercial programs such as Accelerated Reader or Accelerated Math that allow students to work at their own pace, but provide the teacher and student with daily progress updates. They can also be teacher-made with clear and specific directions (portability is a plus).

An example of a center I used with my students was a money center for my fourth graders who were having difficulty counting coins and making change. One activity included a puzzle I had made where students matched cards with coins to corresponding dollar amounts. When they were done they would turn the entire puzzle over and if they had completed the activity correctly the puzzle would show a picture of a dollar bill.

Another activity was cooperative in that it included menus from different local restaurants and students would take turns playing the waiter and the customer and would have to figure out the total bill including tax and gratuity. They could then check their work with a calculator and submit the receipts to me.

Making learning centers fun and changing them regularly keeps students interested and allows the teacher additional time to work with smaller groups of students. Effective time management is another survival skill that enables me to effectively deal with increases in class size.

As an exceptional student education teacher I am constantly attending individualized education plan conferences, planning for individual student learning goals, teaching my students, and keeping up with my other professional responsibilities. Add this to a balanced life with family, friends, and professional and personal growth and it can be very overwhelming.

There may never seem to be enough time to do what needs to be done. I have always tried to make sure that when I am with my students they have my undivided attention. Class time is not the time to do all that needs doing. That being said, I once read a book by Susan Trott called *The Holy Man* that includes the following quote:

> Realize you have at least an extra hour everyday, probably four, in which to learn a language or calculus. Use your mind to the hilt. Life passes quickly and toward the end gathers speed like a freight train running downhill. The more you know, the more you enrich yourself and others.

I agree completely with Susan Trott and I have changed my perception of what good planning means. A to-do list is useless because too often we do the easy items first and never do the important or meaty tasks on the list just so that we can cross off a bunch of little things and convince ourselves that we were productive.

The simple fact of prioritizing items and breaking large tasks into smaller ones makes a tremendous difference. It has allowed me to do all that I need to do and schedule and do all that I want to do. As a teacher I take a few minutes each day in the morning or evening to plan and to review and this makes all the difference.

There are many systems in place to assist teachers in planning and organizing their time, such as Franklin Covey or Daytimer, and my advice is to pick one and personalize it. No matter how many students are in my class I can be sure that I am doing the best that I can for them through effective planning and organization. Effective time management and learning centers have helped me to handle changes in class size and load.

Teaching in a Multiage Classroom

LYNN CLARK

Joes, Colorado

Two years ago I had a major change in my classroom when I went from my comfortable second-grade position to a combination classroom of second and third graders. Ours is a small rural school of approximately 100 students registered in Grades K-12, and we are getting smaller by the year. When I was a student at Liberty School 20 years ago, we averaged 15 students per grade level.

At the end of this past year, our high school classes averaged ten students per class, our junior high eight, and our elementary classes averaged only six students per grade. In the past five years I have taught here, we have cut our elementary staff from six teachers, plus full-time music and art positions, to three full-time elementary teachers plus two other teachers who teach in the classroom half-time and teach either music or art half-time.

Because of these cutbacks, we have found it necessary to combine grade levels. Beginning next year, we will have kindergarten alone, but will combine first and second grades with one teacher, third and fourth grades with another teacher, and fifth and sixth grades with a third teacher. Although our total numbers are still low, we have found some special problems that come with trying to teach two distinct grade levels at once.

After two years with a second-third grade combination, I will be moving to a third-fourth grade combination and at the same time I will be making some major changes in my teaching style to better accommodate teaching two grade levels at once.

These past two years I have tried to maximize my time with each of my classes by alternating their music, art, and physical education classes, so that while one class was out of the room, I would work with the other group. I felt like the students were getting the education they needed, but a day without breaks was nearly more than I could take, and doing all my prep and grading outside of class was making for a very long day.

During other times of the day, I tried to teach two separate lessons at the same time. I would start one grade on a math lesson and then leave them to continue while I started the other grade level.

This was never a very satisfactory situation, as I was never fully available to answer questions for either group. I have been thinking and rethinking these situations over for two years, and I am ready now to put some changes into place that will enable me to teach both grades at the same time, while still addressing the appropriate Colorado Standards.

Some subjects are easier than others to deal with in a combination class. We address social studies and science standards by alternating between the third- and fourth-grade curricula. This way, by the time the students leave my room, they will have had both curricula, although they may have been taught in the wrong order!

We will address handwriting as an independent exercise, with each grade working in its own workbook, which works well since both grades learned cursive in second grade. Our handwriting is mostly practice with few new skills to be presented. My two classes will continue to have art two days a week, one class at a time, which will give me time to have a guided reading lesson with only half the students in the room.

Since time is always a precious commodity, I have made a decision to address reading comprehension strategies and writing practice during our social studies and science time. As we address the content of the social studies and science topics, we will also discuss the strategies we use to comprehend what we read. We will practice strategies for improving the content and style of our writing by responding to what we read, writing reports, recording and reporting data, and summarizing our reading.

I was fortunate, while attending a conference last spring, to see a sample lesson plan for individual spelling lessons, and I have decided to take this approach for my spelling next year. There are quite a few similarities between the spelling lists of the third and fourth grades in the spelling series that our district has adopted, so I have combined the lists.

Following a pretest, each student and I will choose a list of 10 words that he or she would like to work on over the coming week. The students will have the opportunity to study at home and at school, both alone and in pairs. I have been collecting various teacher resource books that give suggestions for games that can be used with any spelling list.

The students will then pair up at the end of the week to give each other a spelling test, which will save me from trying to make three or four spelling lists at the same time for a Friday test! We will cover another part of the curriculum by addressing phonics skills right along with our spelling lessons.

The assessments that accompany our district's reading series address many literacy skills that we can't cover with reading comprehension during science and social studies time or during our phonics and spelling time. Fortunately, many of these skills are similar for both third and fourth grades, so they can be taught at the same time.

This brings me to math, which is the subject that I've had the most trouble trying to integrate. I have found it hard to find an easy correlation between the textbooks at the two grade levels, even though they come from the same series. This led me to the realization that I may need to rely less on the textbook for our daily work, keeping it as a resource so we continue to have a solid curriculum, but not relying on it solely for our math lessons.

At the same time, I have become convinced of the need to address problem-solving skills in math, rather than simply learn facts. After correlating the two texts, I found 18 areas that need to be addressed in the math curriculum. Some will be more of an emphasis for third grade and some more for fourth, but all are areas that need to be covered by both classes. I have listed the Colorado State Standards for both grades and will use these standards to plan lessons that will be flexible enough to cover two different levels.

Putting all the above information together, I am looking for math lessons with a real hands-on, problem-solving element and lessons that are flexible enough to cover two grade levels and that cover the Colorado State Standards.

I was lucky enough to receive an Ernest Duncan Grant from the National Council of Teachers of Mathematics to help with the expense of modifying my math curriculum. The focus of the grant is professional development, and my expenditures will be in three different areas.

Part of my plan to help me reorganize will be attending a math conference and participating in as many sessions as possible that deal with problem solving, multiage classrooms, or hands-on math. Another part of my plan is to observe other multiage classrooms, especially those that teach without relying on a textbook. The third part will be to purchase as many texts and resources as possible to give us a variety of lessons to choose from.

I'm sure with all these changes that will take place that my school year will be an exciting, intense one. I'm looking forward to this, and I'm looking forward to seeing the results that these new ideas have on student learning.

A Community of Learners

LUIS SORIA

Chicago, Illinois

U npredictable mandate changes remain controversial as pundits fail to grasp the fundamental concept that children are more than a singular frame of mind at a given point in time during their education. Children are also more than a lump sum of their experiences, feelings, understandings, and histories. Innately wise and realistic, children are more than blank slates from birth.

How children learn involves the entire package. The package, then, must incorporate how to learn within a community of learners. It is little wonder that the National Board for Professional Teaching Standards includes "Building a Classroom Community" as a crucial component for accomplished teachers. Student choice and voice are critical but not infallible. Educators begin with this premise and facilitate learning to honor student input when establishing the classroom environment.

In my classroom, students belong to a learning community that is collaborative, cooperative, nurturing, and respectful. To create this learning environment, I first develop a sense of community among the students and recognize the diversity of their past classroom and life experiences. By providing opportunities for discourse related to classroom life, my students strengthen their ability to communicate as they consider the perspectives and expectations of behavior from their peers. My students build on their successful strategies to interact positively when they participate in meaningful conversations.

To facilitate collaboration among my students, I randomly arrange groups of four to five students on the first day of class. My current students have experienced classrooms that stressed rote memorization of classroom rules and sat in rows, in isolation. They tell me they rarely collaborated because "it was cheating" to help someone in class. Student talk was limited to short-answer responses to teacher-generated questions.

Although most of the students have known each other since kindergarten, many were uncomfortable sitting together in small groups because they had no prior experience with this classroom setting. During the first few days of class, others misunderstood the seating arrangement as an opportunity to be disruptive during the day. My students had not created a shared history or community in order to interact collaboratively.

Therefore, to initiate cooperative discussions and to create a socially supportive and positive environment, my students had to first shape our classroom governance together. To provide student input in our class governance, my students create a "class compact" to establish guidelines for their social and academic interactions and responsibilities.

This compact is developed over a period of several days and has often led to hour-long discussions due to the high interest of making our own rules and developing our own consequences. In their small groups, the students take turns discussing their expectations for themselves, each other, and me. They listen to each other and are encouraged to agree or disagree (with an explanation) for each point that is shared.

When my students are required to have an explanation for a disagreement, they become less combative and more respectful of what the other group members are willing to share. This occurs because they understand that a group member might disagree with a point they are making. Students have shared that they were less anxious to speak their opinions and less eager to disagree for the sake of disagreeing.

Each student becomes willing to take risks because the active listeners are motivated to understand the primary focus, which is to create the classroom guidelines within a safe environment. My role as the facilitator is to listen to suggestions, when invited by a group, and ask for another group member's opinion. I avoid sharing my input because I want the students to understand that they are constructing their own learning environment and the framework that guides the proponents of their interactions.

After the initial discussion sessions, the small groups of students then make lists of their shared guidelines on large chart paper. They are listed as positive statements, for example, "Do . . . " as opposed to "Do not. . . . " I encourage them to avoid oppressive language to avoid any negative connotations to the process.

I plan for them to understand that these guidelines are an intrinsic barometer for their social interactions and not an extrinsic form for rewarded behavior. Each group places their chart paper on a classroom wall. All group members take turns to explain their rationale for classroom behavior and expectations.

When sharing their insights, my students are surprised by what they have in common. This first-week activity begins to build a community within the classroom. They recognize that, although they have different academic levels, strengths, and perspectives, their expectations for respect and understanding are very similar. This powerful tool for class governance empowers the students to feel comfortable and to listen to each other.

During the next stage of the development of the class compact, my students take a walking tour of the charts and carefully reread what each group has written. On large Post-it notes they make suggestions and comments and attach them to the charts. The small groups then read the notes and together edit their charts accordingly.

For the final draft of the class compact, by democratic vote, my students select the expectations and behaviors that best represent our classroom community. If a student, or group of students, feels strongly about a guideline that has been excluded, he or she is encouraged to discuss with the class why it should be included. Each time this has occurred, the students have chosen to include the guideline that was originally excluded.

Again, the listeners and the speakers are motivated to create the conventions that govern our classroom because they understand that their opinions are valued and validated by the class compact. After completing the compact, each member of the classroom community signs it, including me, and we prominently display it in our room. The students often refer to it when another student has not complied with the structure that was created.

When a student has consistently not complied with our class compact, he or she may be brought to a class meeting by a student or me. Our weekly class meetings last approximately 20 minutes or until all issues are resolved. Class meetings are designed to assist students and me with conflict resolution.

While the discussions are spontaneous and varied each week, we follow a structured format to develop a routine that is comfortable for our class family. Seated in a circle, we face each other as the meeting is called to order by a student. Students rotate weekly to convene our meetings.

We begin our class meetings with acknowledgments. Students are encouraged to thank someone in class for a gesture or favor that was performed. At first, the students did not know what, or how, to acknowledge because they were unfamiliar with this community-building strategy. They usually thanked someone for sharing a pen or a sheet of paper. Beyond that, the students were reluctant to say more and giggling ensued. But that quickly changed.

One afternoon a shy and timid student dropped his lunch tray in the cafeteria. While other classroom students pointed and laughed, several of his classmates simply walked over, helped him collect the mess, patted him on the back, and waited for him to return with his new lunch tray. When I walked over to assist, the students assured me that everything was under control.

My colleagues were amazed by the nurturing and caring manner my students displayed. The student's older brother witnessed the embarrassing scene. He later shared with me that his brother had suggested he acknowledge his classmates for their help during a class meeting.

At our next class meeting, the student who dropped his lunch tray, who had not spoken at all during our previous meetings, acknowledged our class for not laughing at him. He explained that he was very embarrassed. The conversation that followed was an outpouring of embarrassing moments from other students and me that had us laughing. After that meeting, the students acknowledged every sort of kind gesture. "Thanks for walking with me to school . . . for being my friend . . . for helping me with math . . . for editing my paper."

They were comfortable taking new risks because this community-building strategy had reassured them that they were a part of a learning environment that will encourage them to care about each other and to feel safe when mistakes happen.

These mistakes are brought to attention during the next section of our class meeting format. I encourage my students to refer to mistakes or issues and never to problems with another student because that student might feel attacked. The wording for the offense must include, "When you . . . I feel. . . ." This statement identifies how the offended person feels and encourages the offender to understand that he or she is responsible for that feeling.

My students have the opportunity to share information and ideas, to challenge another student's behavior, and to suggest alternatives to an inappropriate behavior. These responsibilities provide positive reinforcement to our class compact.

My students are learning to be responsible to each other because they have the responsibility to shape the conventions that govern our interactions with each other. When students are challenged for not complying with our compact, they have the opportunity to listen to the challenger, another student or me, to ask questions about the issue, and then to either defend or explain their own point of view.

Usually a student will admit his or her mistake and apologize. The student convener will then ask for suggestions to avoid this mistake in the future. My students then share their ideas or similar experiences and how they resolved the mistake. At times, there have been tears and major misunderstandings.

Some students are completely unaware they have committed an offense to a fellow classmate and are sincerely apologetic, offering a hug or a handshake. When the students have agreed that the issue is resolved, the student mediator asks if there are any other issues in the class. When our meeting is adjourned the students return to their small groups with a positive attitude, smiling and hugging each other.

My students work on issues in a climate of social and emotional support. They construct their own governance with my guidance and make a commitment to follow it. They are not alienated or disengaged from the process of the class guidelines but rather are active participants in developing socially positive attitudes that will have an impact on their future interactions.

The older brother is an excellent example of this impact, remembering to acknowledge a good deed in a class meeting three years after participating in the process. Alfie Kohn, in his book *No Contest: The Case Against Competition*, states that "a structure of positive interdependence (your success equals my success) inclines us to look more favorably on the people with whom we are interacting than a structure of negative interdependence (your success equals my failure)."

The social interactions that occur in our class are defined by the positive reinforcement that my students give each other. When one student is successful, they have all participated in the success because they care about each other. Unlike their past experiences, they are not responsible for following my rules but rather are accountable to fulfill a commitment they made to our learning community.

In her article "Another Look at What Young Children Should Be Learning," Lillian Katz identifies feelings as a learning goal. She states, "Among feelings that are learned are those of competence, confidence, belonging and security." In a positive, caring environment, students learn from each other to acquire and strengthen these feelings. My students feel competent to formulate and implement our class guidelines and to confidently share their experiences.

They belong to a community that recognizes their strengths and provides the security to address their needs. They are engaged when they interact with each other and they actively listen to each other's opinions. They are not passive participants, but eager sharers of feelings and personal interpretations.

My students take ownership in the expectations and outcomes for their behavior and therefore initiate the changes that occur to the conventions that govern our classroom. They collaborate to amend our class compact as needed. One example of an amendment to our compact is the inclusion of student input for scoring rubrics.

My students were unfamiliar with scoring rubrics at the beginning of the year. Once the students and their parents understand this form of assessment, I begin to ask for their input on a few assignments. Two months into the school year, one student asked, "Why can't we say how many points we need for a high score?" Other students agreed. I took advantage of this "teachable moment" to explain class compact amendments.

My students followed the same procedures, collaborating and sharing their ideas, as when they created the original compact. After two days of discussion, they decided to amend our class compact with, "When possible, the students will choose how many points are given for at least two sections of scoring rubrics."

The debate over "when possible" and "always" was hotly contested. My students listened respectfully to each other and collaboratively made compromises for the amendment. Now they are responsible for their own governance, social interactions, and assessments of learning and growth over time. I expect they will continue to make amendments over the course of the year.

Another change I expect will be the ability to further apply class meeting strategies to their lives. My students will see the positive effect of meaningful discussions in their social interactions. They will take further responsibility for their actions and understand how these actions influence the classroom community and their lives outside of the classroom.

During a recent home visit, a student's mother said her daughter shares her feelings on a daily basis. She said, "My daughter walks around saying, 'I'm upset because you . . . ' or 'I feel sad when she. . . .'" Her mother found it reaffirming that her daughter had "come out of her shell" to explicitly detail how she felt and why she felt that way.

My students are creating these changes in their lives, in and out of the classroom, because they now have the tools to take on the responsibility that governs their actions.

Each year, colleagues in my school comment on the nurturing way my students treat each other. Recently the music teacher said, "It can't be because you're getting the good students every year! What are you feeding these kids? How do you do it every year?" I honor their dignity. I recognize that my students have a wealth of information to share.

They are not blank slates, but rich, full vessels who deserve the opportunity to share what is on their minds. They are safe to reveal themselves during class meetings and throughout the day. They practice democracy when they create their class compact and value each other's input. They collaboratively reach agreements as they challenge each other to recognize the humanity of each person in the classroom, including me.

This stimulating environment invigorates the students to feel as though they belong to a special place. They eagerly anticipate being in a classroom that fosters their sense of community.

So, while the "experts" continue to change national, state, and local standards, alter the curriculum annually, and make further demands on standardized tests, the ongoing thread in a best-practice environment must include a community of learners. With this essential component well established, changes (minute or significant) will have a less-negative impact on your family of learners.

Who Says Standards Have to Be Boring?

Rosalyn L. Pollard

Westland, Michigan

It is a challenge to provide students with meaningful learning experiences while adhering to the guidelines and mandates we as teachers find ourselves working under. As a teacher working with students with special needs, most of whom have difficulty with reading and written language, it is an additional challenge to teach language arts.

By sixth grade many students have found both reading and writing to be terribly frustrating. It's the last thing they want to do. I have found that using the standards established by my state as my foundation, combined with a content of student interests and a variety of instructional resources, is the key to meeting the challenge.

The English language arts standards for my state are written in broad and general terms. Draft benchmarks are provided in a curriculum framework document. I use the curriculum framework to shape thematic units and classroom activities. I teach middle school students, sixth grade to be specific. Each group is different so content and plans change from year to year to meet both the needs and the interests of the students. Instructional resources may include printed materials, community resources, and technology.

One year a ferret was adopted as a class pet. Neither my students nor myself knew very much about ferrets. An outgrowth of the desire to learn more about our new class pet and the interest in pets in general led to the development of a thematic unit entitled "Responsible Pet Ownership and

Animal Rescues." During the course of the unit student activities included the following:

- Reading a variety of sources, including newspaper articles and magazine articles, and responding to the plight of animals (1.1) (The numbers in parentheses refer to the standards listed below.)
- Viewing videotapes to gain information on ferret care and the plight of retired greyhounds (1.5)
- Searching the Internet for information on Rainbow Bridge and how others deal with the death of a pet—this followed the death of another classroom pet (1.5)
- Writing thank-you notes to guest speakers (2.1)
- Writing three forms of poetry—pet names and haiku following the theme and free verse from the point of view of a homeless animal on the street and the same animal once it has been adopted into a loving home (2.1)
- Writing a persuasive essay on animal adoption (2.1)
- Conducting group interviews with community resources—humane society representatives or greyhound rescue and ferret rescue volunteers (3.3)

Independent reading provides an opportunity to uphold standards in my classroom (7.3). I utilize an independent reading program in my classroom, which allows students to take computerized tests on selected books for points. I set the goal for my students for the first semester. My students set their own goals for the second semester. They keep track of their goals by utilizing an independent reading log. Individual conferences are held during the semester.

Inquiry (Content Standard 8) can take different forms. One inquiry involved an investigation to determine how certain aromas affected one's ability to study. The inquiry was based on information from *Brain Based Learning* by Eric Jensen. A second inquiry involved students working in teams to plan, organize, and conduct taste tests on peers to determine favorite chocolate candy bars. Their conclusions were reported to different sixth-grade advisory groups.

Standards are not to be feared. In my classroom, they provide a foundation on which to build a challenging and engaging learning environment with activities geared toward students' interests.

Content Standard 1. All students will read and comprehend general and technical material.

> 1.1. Use reading for multiple purposes such as enjoyment, clarifying information, and learning complex procedures.

> 1.2. Employ multiple strategies to construct meaning, such as generating questions, studying vocabulary, analyzing mood and tone, recognizing how authors use information, generalizing ideas, matching form to content, and developing reference skills.

> 1.5. Respond to a variety of oral, visual, written, and electronic texts by making connections to their personal lives and the lives of others.

Content Standard 2. All students will demonstrate the ability to write clear and grammatically correct sentences, paragraphs, and compositions.

> 2.1. Write fluently for multiple purposes to produce compositions, such as personal narratives, persuasive essays, lab reports, and poetry.

> 2.2. Recognize and use authors' techniques that convey meaning and build empathy with readers when composing their own texts.

Content Standard 3. All students will focus meaning and communications as they listen, speak, view, read, and write in personal, social, occupational, and civic contexts.

> 3.3. Read and write fluently, speak confidently, listen and interact appropriately, view critically, and represent creatively.

Content Standard 7. All students will demonstrate, analyze, and reflect upon the skills and processes used to communicate through listening, speaking, viewing, reading, and writing.

    7.3. Reflect on their own developing literacy, set learning goals, and evaluate their progress.

Content Standard 8. All students will define and investigate important issues and problems using a variety of resources, including technology, to explore and create texts.

    8.1. Generate questions about important issues that affect them or topics about which they are curious, narrow the questions to a clear focus, and create a thesis or a hypothesis.

    8.2. Explain and use resources that are most appropriate and readily available for investigating a particular question or topic.

    8.3. Organize, analyze, and synthesize information to draw conclusions and implications based on their investigation of an issue or problem.

    8.4. Use different means of developing and presenting conclusions based on the investigation of an issue or problem to an identified audience.

Inclusion of New Populations

AVALYN BALLIET

Irving, Texas

Inclusion is a word that means many different things to me—to include, to involve, to bring into the circle those who were left out previously (being a history teacher,

Plessy v. Ferguson always comes to mind when thinking on the premise of separate but equal). The connotation is that of welcoming or being given permission to join a community.

Ideally, everyone has experienced the joy of joining a group where you feel welcomed and have a sense of belonging—whether that be a family, a church, a support group, a circle of friends, or a network of colleagues—but there is also trepidation at the new prospect of change. Am I up to the challenge? Will they accept me? What will be required of me? We all ask these questions, and our students ask them, too.

Inclusion is a new buzzword in my school district. Except for a small fraction of our student population, we have changed from self-contained special education classrooms to mainstreaming most students into general education classrooms. Additionally, all students, whether their handicapping condition is mental retardation, autism, or emotional disturbance, are with the general population during advisory or in an elective class.

This is a major paradigm shift in traditional special education, but we recognize that all students can learn and will learn when given the opportunity to be included. It is not easy. Of the eighth graders sitting in my U.S. history classroom, I have had a child with Down syndrome next to a "gifted and talented" student beside an "honors" kid who is near a student who used to be in "resource" special ed and across from a "regular" kid whose single mom cannot afford to buy him glasses and who is surrounded by students who arrived here from another country within the past two years and are struggling to master conversational English in addition to academic language. Whew! Did I mention that my school is 68% Hispanic, 78% minority, 31% ESL, and 73% economically disadvantaged? How do you include all those different types of kids? How do you make sure all students are learning and that no one gets left behind?

Well, I start by ensuring that all activities and strategies are student-focused and objective-based. I consciously work at remembering and imagining my students' frame of reference regarding concepts, skills, and schema. They are entering a classroom with varying abilities and multiple intelligences. Therefore, I must teach in a multiplicity of formats and approaches. For my inclusion special ed students, I work very closely with my team's inclusion specialist (formerly a special ed teacher) on modifications, planning, progress reports, and individual education plans (IEPs). For my inclusion ESL students, I use strategies that are built on visual or kinesthetic styles or that require social interaction to build vocabulary such as cooperative learning.

By teaching the text backward (learned in a workshop by Judy Jameson), I start with the application to daily life or experiential exercise, then go backward to discussions, video clips, and finally worksheets or graphic organizers and reading the text. These strategies are not only excellent for the so-called new populations, but the old populations thrive with them as well. It is good for *all* kids. Inclusion can be successful when you truly believe that all children can learn.

Parents: A Natural Resource

CINDY ALBERT

Caribou, Maine

We all know that parents are a child's first teacher. Why is it, then, that parents were virtually forbidden from entering the schools or classrooms until quite recently? Educators were missing out on one of the most invaluable resources for educating the children in our communities. Millennium educators are now realizing that we need to tap into this precious natural resource.

As a former multiage teacher of children ages 5 to 7, I most certainly took advantage of every parental involvement opportunity that arose. Volunteerism had many faces. Some parents volunteered by donating necessary items to the classroom. Each year I posted a "giving tree" at our annual open house. Parents were given the opportunity to take "apples" from the tree and send in the listed materials. It's amazing how much they are willing to give, as long as you tell them exactly what is needed, from games to tissue paper. Periodically throughout the year, our weekly parent letter listed various items that needed to be replenished or that would be necessary for children to participate in a particular learning experience. Once again, our parents were there for us.

Other parents donated their time by making or creating learning materials at home, which were subsequently used in the classroom. Many parents were not aware of how they could help with their child's education. Once we explained the variety of contributions, they were continually asking for more ways to help. Still other parents volunteered by chaperoning occasional field trips or attending special functions.

Yet another extremely valuable form of volunteerism is the gift of time spent within the school with the children. At the beginning of each school year, I skimmed through my class list looking for parental occupations that would lend themselves well to finding available time to come into the classroom during the school day. These parents were then contacted individually and asked if they would be willing to become teaching partners in their child's classroom. I also enlisted the aid of older siblings, grandparents, and even neighbors! These volunteers were scheduled on a daily, weekly, or monthly basis depending on the time available.

I took the time to learn more about each parent's strengths and tailored educational activities around him or her. The parents were trained to work with the children individually or in small groups. Each time they came into the classroom they were given a set of directions and all the necessary materials to carry out the lesson. I not only entrusted my parents with the education of the children, but also gave them the appropriate respect.

In so doing, I was able to take on more small group learning activities and develop my skills with the newest teaching strategies and methodologies. Without the assistance of my parents as teaching partners, I would never have been able to teach as many concepts and skills in such a variety of ways that met the individual needs of each child in my classroom. Parents not only increased the teacher-child ratio but they also became excellent teachers in their own right.

There is an old proverb, "If you give a man a fish, you feed him for a day. If you teach a man to fish, you feed him for a lifetime." The same can be said of children and their parents. When I teach a child, I am only reaching that child. However, when I take the time to teach a parent to teach, then I'm touching many lives for many years to come.

By building such strong home-school relations, I also increased the parental attendance at numerous other school-related functions. As I look back on my past few years in multi-age, I can't imagine doing it alone, nor would I ever want to again.

Parents quickly became a necessary staple in my classroom. Without them I could not deliver the quality education that was being demanded of me. Invest in your parents, show your belief in them, compliment them, trust them, and acknowledge the many gifts they have to share. Parents are a natural resource that can literally make our jobs easier.

Math, Science, and Technology in the Next Millennium

Change Can Be a Good Thing

GERALD FRIDAY

Milwaukee, Wisconsin

When I am asked, "What is the number one quality a teacher needs to have to be successful?" my answer is that a successful teacher needs to deal with change. Change is something that will always be a part of your teaching environment. In my situation, I had put together a successful program for teaching biology to our high school sophomores. It was a program that I enjoyed teaching and that generated success and interest within my students.

The sophomores who were enrolled in biology had taken general science when they were freshmen. The general science program at our school was one that we as a science department faculty were not completely pleased with. Since we draw students from a large number of community grade schools, the students' science backgrounds varied considerably. It was this variance that created the problems for us.

Since we have an accelerated and a general track for our students, it was very difficult to correctly place students in the course that was best suited for them. Adding to this problem was the pressure from parents to have their children skip general science because of their grade school science background. This, unfortunately, led to numerous placement errors, which made the experience of learning science not very enjoyable for the students involved.

Our solution was to drop the general science program and move biology and chemistry down one grade level. Physics still remained as a senior course. This provided new opportunities for the pupils during their junior year, allowing us to provide advanced placement biology and chemistry to qualified students. It also allowed us to create a course for those students not accepted into the advanced placement program that would give them a broader knowledge of biology and chemistry.

The new junior course would consist of a semester of continuing topics in chemistry and a semester of biology. We decided as a department that since the biology teachers always seemed to fall short of covering a unit on ecology, the semester of biology should be centered on the study of our biological environment.

But who would teach this course? My science department agreed it should be none other than me. They stated that I was a motivating and creative teacher who would stand up to the challenge of developing a new course. There I was, a teacher who loves biology, a teacher who takes summer courses to advance his knowledge in the various topics of biology, but who for some reason had avoided the topic of ecology.

A negative experience with a plant taxonomy course in college led me to shy away from plant courses. Since that course, any class that had plants listed in its description was eliminated from my list of courses to enroll in. Unfortunately, there are no descriptions of ecology that don't mention plants. Thus, after about 50 credits in various topics of biology, none being in ecology, I was going to teach ecology. Yikes! What a change from what I had been doing!

My first task was to blank out my past experience in taxonomy and begin reading articles and books on ecology. I even enrolled in various workshops to learn more about our environment and to begin designing a curriculum for my new course. The way I perceived the situation was that I didn't have time to worry about my circumstances. I was going to have a room full of students wanting to learn about environmental biology in a few months.

It turns out that teaching ecology has been the greatest experience. What is interesting about environmental science is that it's so pertinent that it's almost impossible not to find an article in the daily newspaper on some topic dealing with our environment. It's also a very integrated subject in that it is greatly affected by the social sciences.

Environmental science is also taught differently from other subjects I've taken. It has an element of action. Environmental science attempts to motivate students to use the knowledge they have acquired. It's not uncommon for the students in an ecology course to participate in car-pooling, recycling, and other stewardship activities.

Since I was going to teach a course about the environment, my goal was to take my students out of school and give them a field experience—not an easy task for a teacher teaching in an urban school surrounded by concrete and blacktop. Fortunately, we do have a river within walking distance from our school.

One of the workshops I had attended was on determining the water quality of a river. I have greatly modified their approach by adding some additional activities that are directed toward the interests of each student and that promote the process of science. These additions have resulted in more student ownership of our study and have provided an opportunity for students to share and interact with each other within a scientific atmosphere.

Our unit begins with a watershed awareness activity in which the students, by way of filling out a survey, are asked questions about the location and water quality of the watershed in which they reside. This leads to many questions that help create an informative discussion. The class is then provided with street and geological maps so that they may determine their watershed by locating the river nearest to their residence. Next, the students transfer this information to a classroom map where they observe the location of the other students' residences and see who else lives in their watershed. This activity provides a great deal of awareness, interest, and sharing.

The classroom map activity also helps me organize the students into groups according to their location within their watershed. The goal is to create teams consisting of two to four pupils. The students are given instructions on how to safely collect water samples and how to analyze them. There are a variety of methods that can be used. For this, I prefer to follow the guidelines of the National Sanitation Foundation, which can be found in most manuals on testing river water quality.

A field trip is planned to provide an opportunity for the students to stop at each of the sites to collect their water samples and examine the water. An extra sample is collected from each site to be later analyzed at school. During our sampling and testing of the water, goggles and plastic gloves are always worn as a safety precaution.

A significant amount of time and care is spent in the classroom lab testing the river water collected from the various field trip sites. Supplemental readings are assigned to help students understand how environmental conditions at various sites can have an effect on water quality. The results of those tests, along with the test data from the field trip, assist the students in calculating the water quality of their site. The hands-on experience of going out into the environment to observe, combined with the classroom work of analyzing and interpreting data, provides the students with a practical yet exciting atmosphere in which they can learn and experience the scientific process.

Once the students have determined the water quality of their site, they are asked to share their results using a scientific format. This is done by writing a scientific paper, complete with tables and charts, and by giving an oral presentation of their paper to the class.

The watershed teams are encouraged to return to their watershed site and examine the area for factors that may have contributed to their water quality findings. A slide camera is made available so students can take pictures of their site's environment. These slides can be used during the group presentations.

Each team portrays their watershed, using maps and slides, so we, the audience, have a good visual picture of what their watershed is like. The data are presented and their significance is explained. The students can hypothesize how the surroundings of their site, such as a forest, golf course, or parking lot, can affect the water quality of the river. By having the students share the results of the numerous sites along the river, students are able to learn about how change in the environment affects the river as it flows from one environmental setting to another.

These activities have fostered student interest in local watersheds and have provided a stimulus for them to become involved in improving local water quality. Many of the students have gone beyond the scope of this project by writing letters to companies along the river, encouraging them to take better care it. Some students have volunteered for river clean-up groups while others have communicated about watershed issues with students from other schools. These students use their acquired knowledge and skills in taking thoughtful, positive action toward the resolution of environmental issues, thus making a contribution to their community.

Success With School Technology

COLLEEN COOPER ASHWORTH

Missoula, Montana

School reform is a hot issue across America and futuristic school leaders are looking for new ways to invoke positive changes. For example, in elementary, middle, and secondary schools today, teachers and their students are becoming more adept at using technological innovations through the use of classroom computers. These educators are not only having tremendous success with their technology programs in their classrooms, but are also sharing this success with their communities.

Unfortunately, not all schools are having success with technology; nor are all communities ready to invest large amounts of money in school technology. Recent studies indicate there are many schools and communities being left behind technologically. Part of the problem is a lack of leadership, awareness, and knowledge as to how technology can best be utilized in schools. For example, many school administrators across the country are saddling teachers with a plethora of mismatched hand-me-down machines, printers, and software that is incompatible and seldom works.

A typical teacher might have one or more computers in the classroom but rarely use them because of the confusion. More than likely, the computers are incompatible, outdated, or need repairs. The existing software is probably game oriented and difficult to tie to the curricula. Little or no quality courseware is designed to provide integrated learning. The result is very frustrated teachers who quickly give up on using technology.

Numerous school administrators have tried to address this problem by installing networked computer labs. This solution worked for some schools but not for all. A primary problem with computer labs is scheduling. Many teachers have difficulty scheduling computer labs into their day-to-day operations.

For example, teachers who generally prefer a more activity-centered environment need instant access to technology that allows them to make quick shifts from direct teaching to cooperative learning strategies. Unless the lab is next door or is not being used, many teachers will not take the time to walk students down the hall or to another building to use a lab. Thus, many teachers across the United States have found computer labs awkward to schedule and not conducive to the teachable moment.

This dilemma has created a debate between administrators and teachers about which is best, the computer lab or the classroom model. Unfortunately, few schools have been able to afford both. The resulting confusion has cost some schools their community support and funding for educational technology.

The quandary over classroom networked computers verses labs, however, seems to be finally turning a corner. Technology planners are now beginning to realize the vast potential for high-speed networked computers in classrooms. They are finding that networked computers in classrooms or laptops allow teachers to reach a wider range of student ability. This is particularly true when trying to accommodate preferred learning styles of individual students.

Using a one to five ratio of computers to students and networking them in classrooms is proving to be one of the most successful ways to integrate technology into schools. In reviewing the literature, educators are finding that technology is making a significant impact in at least five areas other than student achievement: increasing the amount of student writing, increasing the quality of writing, enhancing cooperative learning, enhancing integrated learning, and application of learning styles. The following reflect each area in more detail.

Amount of Student Writing. Simply measuring the amount that students are using computers to write reveals the positive impact of technology. For example, many teachers are finding that students are currently writing up to three times more than they did previously without technology. A keyboard often appears to be less physically demanding for most students to use than a pen or pencil. The result is that students are writing more. This will become even more pronounced with the advent of voice recognition, a new technological application soon to be available to schools.

Quality of Student Writing. Analysis of student writing has shown that word processing does help students become more effective writers. Anyone who uses word processing to any degree can probably agree with this. Students using word processing can check grammar and spelling and rewrite their work many times over with greater ease.

Cooperative Learning. Schools using five networked computers and a printer in classrooms are finding that this format enhances cooperative learning. Using classroom computer centers as learning stations, many teachers are finding it easier to have students work in groups. Allowing students to work in groups within the classroom is the basis for cooperative learning.

Integration of Curriculum. Teachers in their classrooms that have access to the Internet and scanner devices are finding that it is easier to cross-reference and integrate social studies, literature, math, and science. For example, using the Internet, PowerPoint, and Hyper-Studio, students are able to create elaborate presentations utilizing material from multiple disciplines. Maps, graphs, tables, illustrations, and text from many subject areas are easily incorporated into a student research paper or visual presentation.

Application of Learning Styles. Dr. Rita Dunn, Professor at Johns Hopkins University, has shown that there is a significant correlation between the use of technology and the application of student learning styles in the classroom. Dunn points out in her research that computer technology is designed to enhance the use of student visual, auditory, and kinesthetic modalities.

In conclusion, we can see that the five areas noted above do reflect a partial list of the benefits that high-speed networked computers in the classroom can bring to our schools. It is important to note, then, that when children have access to technology in the classroom they become more efficient learners. It is through the development of effective classroom technology that we have the best chance of reforming schools and doing what we do best in education—help children learn.

Introduction of New Technologies

CARMELLA ETTARO

West Hills, California

I have always been interested in learning and implementing new strategies to motivate students to attend class and want to be in my classroom. If they come to class and I can make it a nonthreatening environment, then students can be taught mathematics. My first graphing calculator was bought because of the "big" screen and I liked to see my input.

It wasn't long before a week-long workshop was offered at the county offices on how to use this technology as a teaching tool. At first I thought I would have to retire. I couldn't possibly learn this. The instructor was excellent and encouraged us to attend a "Teachers Teaching With Technology" conference the following spring.

So off I went with three colleagues and, wow, the whole idea of technology took off at my school! The sponsoring company had some of the most outstanding workshop leaders and treated us so professionally. Although I stayed with the beginners, I learned so much that I implemented lessons immediately into my classroom. I have gone back every year. It is a renewal that I look forward to.

As a department chair I had a vision of what a math classroom should look like: double screened, one for an overhead projector and one for the graphing calculator and PC demonstration station. At that time I had a supportive administration both on-site and at the district.

It would be very difficult now to teach without this wonderful, visual, investigative tool. I learned a valuable lesson from a student who entered my Analysis Honors class on petition because he didn't have the grade prerequisite.

He started using the graphing calculator and solved most of the problems visually by graphing. He did extremely well in my class, went on to Advanced Placement Calculus, and earned a perfect score on the exam.

The lesson I learned was that not all students learn and understand math the way I did. I must continually seek out new strategies to reach all students. Kids are different today. Technology is not going away and students use it all the time. We teachers need to remember, especially in mathematics, that not all students see and learn math the way we did. I can teach the parent function $f(x) = x^2$ and proceed to apply translations, stretches, and shrinks.

I am still amazed how students catch on so quickly and then apply it to other functions, including trigonometric ones. This topic was so difficult for a third-year math student when taught in the traditional manner. My innovative unit that won the State Farm Good Neighbor Award is based on technology. Students first investigate classical trigonometry curves, discover their properties, write generic descriptions, design their own curves, and use the Internet for research.

Opposition has been strong at times. I am the first to believe that the basics are required, especially estimation, before using any calculator. As I tell my students, the calculator is only as smart as the person pushing its buttons. The parents most opposed are those who do not recognize the math as how they learned it. These are the same parents who would readily admit they did not like math. Is it some right of passage to subject your child to the same math you did not like? What is the most frustrating is the misuse by teachers who indiscriminately allow calculator use without regard to its appropriateness.

It is much harder to teach with technology since it requires more creative lesson planning and different types of assessment that take longer to grade. As a teacher, I love it best when I am in the classroom and have the opportunity to create lessons and strategies to cause the lightbulb of understanding to go off in my students' eyes. This sustains me for another year of teaching.

The creative and innovative teachers in my department were willing to try the lessons we brought back and to help make my vision a reality. This fall, the last part of my vision was completed and the PC station is in every math classroom. The most recent workshops are now focusing on connecting the real data found on the Internet, downloading to the students' calculators so they can work on real-life applications. My new challenge is to learn how to integrate the Internet and computers into meaningful lessons. A teacher who continues to be a learner survives in this profession.

Students return to visit and tell of the horror stories of not being able to use any type of calculator. High schools are changing, but in many cases colleges are not. We are sending out bright, eager (and in many cases female) students who simply give up mathematics in college because of the way it is taught. We all need to use technology as a motivator: to keep teachers vibrant and enthusiastic, to keep students in math-related careers, and to help adults use mathematics to be numerate.

Reflection Leads to Change

LINDA SEEGER

Milford, Iowa

What makes a successful teacher? If you listen to our departments of education, our legislatures, and some of our administrators, the answer would hinge on how well your students performed on the previous year's standardized tests.

In this new test-driven, results-orientated age of education it seems we've lost our focus on the art of teaching. It is easy to get bogged down in the lingo of our time: standards, benchmarks, multiple assessments, and district and statewide goals for student achievement. The list is endless.

The current educational climate has shifted the focus from the process of educating individual learners-shareholders-students to a results-only justification of the job we do through student test scores. Teachers who will succeed through this latest educational era are those who can strike a balance between the new goal-orientated results and the old passion for student success that first brought us to the classroom.

I obtained National Board Certification in Adolescence and Young Adulthood Mathematics two years ago. This process requires teachers to reflect and discuss their learning practices and strategies as various portfolio items were prepared.

I have continued this self-evaluation process and have continued to reflect daily on my classroom practices. I consider questions such as "How can I make this more understandable?" "What skills need to be built in now, in order to succeed in the next unit?" or "What classroom practices could I change in order to make more efficient use of my time?"

This reflective process proved very valuable when I was faced with teacher accountability through student achievement based on test scores. The Department of Education in Iowa requires that every high school publish a report on its students' achievement on multiple assessments.

Our high school formally publishes reports on student achievement on the Iowa Tests of Educational Development (ITED) and the Okoboji Math Exam (OME). The Okoboji Math Department developed the OME from the standards and benchmarks that we considered literacy level for all high school math students.

Our math department is also informally critiqued on our math ACT scores. I began with the reflective question, "How can I balance what I do in the classroom with the need to score well on standardized tests?" The answer was to change certain classroom practices.

I began using several ACT preparation booklets as regular supplements to my classroom. After every scheduled unit assessment in my Algebra II class the students were required to complete a 10- to 20-question standardized test practice exam (one test approximately every two weeks).

Instead of having downtime after a unit test the students were engaged in practicing standardized test questions. We reviewed the answers the next day and picked out several problems to discuss test-taking strategies and practices to use to solve these problems. By the end of the school year we had done somewhere between 150 and 200 ACT-type problems. The early results are very encouraging as we examine the ACT scores of the students in my classes.

I again put the reflective process to work this spring by asking, "What else can I do to increase student understanding of the concepts presented on the ACT, the ITED, and the OME?" I have chosen to address this issue by adding a journaling element to my Algebra II class next fall. For each class I will have between one and four problems on the board as the students come into the room.

One will be an ACT practice problem and one will be either a practice problem coming from one of the benchmarks on the ITED or from the OME. The other two will be problems from previous concepts covered in the class. These problems will *not* be the actual test problems, just like the ACT practice problems are not the actual test problems. I believe if we are going to hold kids accountable for this information we should provide plenty of classroom practice without teaching them the actual test.

The changes in school climate are being brought about by new demands for teacher accountability on both state and local levels. Reflection can be a valuable aid in creating new strategies to assist teachers in maintaining top quality classrooms while keeping the focus on student-centered learning.

Helpful Tips

I have had much success in teaching Algebra II by forgoing the traditional chapter tests in favor of shorter assessments covering two or three learner objectives that are tied back to a benchmark. Instead of a traditional unit test in which each idea may have one or two test questions, my Algebra II assessments have four to five questions covering each critical concept that builds the students' skills as they progress to Precalculus.

This method helps to avoid that February black hole where students cannot remember the concepts and skills taught early in the school year. My students are aware that if it's a critical objective they will need to use that math skill again in this course and beyond. It helps to make them active partners in their own learning by identifying what must be learned for future use. It is also easy to keep the information fresh in their minds as their teacher revisits briefly these critical concepts throughout the year.

Going Bookless in Earth Science

SHARON JEFFERY

Plymouth, Massachusetts

My undergraduate education courses had insisted that any "good" teacher taught to very dear and measurable objectives. Those first few years, I wrote objective after objective as I taught my eighth-grade Earth Science course. But I was never confident that I was teaching what would be most important for my students to know. I naively figured that if they put it in the textbook I should teach it. That is, until I found myself wondering too often "Why do they need to know that?" Just as I was facing this personal dilemma the state of Massachusetts decided to reform education.

Plymouth's Science Coordinator foresaw the change that would be coming and chose to be one step ahead of the transformation. He asked any interested teachers to meet over the summer and give our input on the state's draft of the new science standards. I volunteered immediately! A group of about 30 science teachers from grades K-12 met for 12 hours to read, edit, and rewrite these proposed standards.

We divided them by topics. We divided them by grade ranges. We eventually rewrote the entire K-12 science curriculum based on these very specific standards. This new curriculum changed my Earth Science to an Integrated Science course. This change in standards and subject area was just the recharge my teaching needed!

I got ready to teach my new eighth-grade curriculum. With standards that were so concrete and so easily assessable, my lessons almost wrote themselves! The only real problem was a lack of adequate background knowledge in biology. Immediately I got a few textbooks to brush up enough to start the year with confidence. Then I enrolled in a college course to beef up my biology education. Over the course of the year I attended three conferences which also gave me more information and ideas to fill out my science wisdom.

Now my big problem was what to leave out! I knew my students needed to do more than learn a bunch of unrelated facts, words, and ideas. I needed to hang my topics on real-life problems or ideas. But what I wanted to teach wasn't in our books. So I wrote quite a few lessons to supplement the book. Then I wrote a whole unit that wasn't even in the book.

Eventually I was using the book so seldom that I actually collected them in April and never used them again that year. Word of this spread throughout the student body and eventually to my fellow teachers. This new idea was very suspect to say the least and caused some heated discussions. How will you review for tests? How can you outline the chapter if they can't take the book home? How can they define the vocabulary? What will a substitute teacher do for work? Questions followed questions. But I was giving answers!

Due to increasing numbers of students and a changing curriculum, the school was hesitant to buy another 75 books that would be used only one more year. The budgets were tight and the available money would be better spent on lab supplies. I went to the Science Coordinator and volunteered to only use a class set of books. After determining that I would be fulfilling the letter of the law (each child will have access to a textbook), he agreed I could try it for the year.

Going bookless has been the best decision I was ever allowed to make. This one change led me to rethink and revamp homework assignments to make them more family oriented and more "real." It allowed me to go in exactly the direction I want on a topic without being bound by a canned program. My assessments have been altered tremendously! No longer do we have the test at the end of the chapter, but now I can constantly gauge where my students are both formally and informally. I learned to survey my students for interests that I could tie in to our topics. I have amended and overhauled my notebook requirements and writing requirements.

Without the confinement of a text I have found integrating and adding technology to be a breeze. My facts and student information are gathered from magazines, television shows, and the Internet. This is science from life, not from a book!

For the first time I felt empowered to really teach. I was guided and bound by the standards, but the path to successful student learning was mine to pave.

Science Teaching Is a Profession—Not a Job!

MARY HARRIS

St. Louis, Missouri

In 1985, I thought I was a good teacher. By that time, I had more than 15 years of experience in three school districts.

Students could pass my exams, nobody was complaining, and I was fairly comfortable with my performance. I decided to apply for a summer institute for middle-level teachers at Princeton University to improve my understanding of science and teaching skills. Drastic changes to my teaching career resulted from this single decision.

A group of us from the institute valued our newfound friendships and wanted to promote an organization that would help the neglected, middle-level science teachers. The formation of the National Middle Level Science Teachers Association (NMLSTA) began with this group of teachers and with others active in the National Science Teachers Association (NSTA).

I volunteered to be the editor of a newsletter and continued in that position for 10 years. As editor, I read and critiqued contributions from teachers all over the country, searched for professional opportunities, developed e-mail dialogues, and wrote about science for the middle level. All of these experiences have made me a better teacher.

Alone in our classrooms each of us works to improve how students respond to curricula we write. But improvement can be even more rapid if we take advantage of good ideas that other teachers have developed and found successful in their classrooms. This is the reason teachers need to be involved in professional organizations.

Of course, a lot of what you hear and see at professional meetings won't work in your classroom, but the innovative ideas make the effort worthwhile. At the same time, there is also a feeling of satisfaction when a fellow teacher adopts one of your good ideas.

The demands on a teacher make it very difficult to find time for professional activities, if they are viewed as an extra responsibility. But those out-of-school commitments are what differentiate an employee from a professional. Giving of oneself and taking risks are behaviors we encourage in our students, so why not take this advice and reach out to peers?

In my own case, one professional responsibility has led to another. Due to my involvement in NMLSTA, I was introduced to the education outreach person for the American Plastics Council (APC). As a result of our conversations, I was asked to form a committee to design the Hands On Plastics kit. Over 30,000 kits have been distributed to teachers, free of charge, in the past six years. Amazingly, this kit works well with students in Grades 6-12 and even college. Go to www.teachingplastics. org and order yours!

Middle-level science teaching was not my goal as I worked on my BS and MAT. I planned to be a high school chemistry teacher but I soon developed an interest and a passion for teaching chemistry at all levels. My current teaching is split between eighth and tenth graders. For the middle-level students, I try to emphasize both science and study skills embedded with chemistry content. My high school students get a rigorous course in chemistry (including two double-period laboratories per week). Both ages know me for my sense of humor, my fairness, and my love of science.

To help me with my high school classes, I belong to the American Chemical Society—St. Louis Topical Group (ACS), the Division of Chemical Education, the National Science Teachers Association, and the Science Teachers of Missouri. These organizations publish journals or newsletters filled with helpful hints and research about science education. My laboratory program is filled with problem-based explorations taken from articles published in these journals.

My demonstrations are largely those that I have read or seen at conventions for NSTA, ACS, ChemEd, or Biennial Conferences on Chemical Education. I make time to read and occasionally write for professional journals and attend as many conventions as I can afford. I feel that I am continuing to grow as a teacher and a person every year I teach.

An exciting extracurricular activity that resulted from my membership in NSTA was participation in ExploraVision. I have had three teams in three years win national recognition for their visions of the future. The visions that my students wanted to pursue involved science ideas that were far removed from my formal college studies.

As I encouraged them to learn and explore their ideas, I became a student of science along with these creative young people. I am now a regional judge of this international K-12 competition. I encourage every teacher to look into this contest at the NSTA Web site (www.nsta.org).

The Hands On Plastics project led to my work, for the past five years, with the Polymer Ambassadors. This is a group of teachers who have been selected by the Intersociety Polymer Education Council to promote polymer education. Learning about polymers and the polymer industry has inspired me to collaborate with other Ambassadors to write teaching modules on macromolecules, food packing, polymer factories, athletic shoes, and elastomers. I am currently developing a Web site for the Ambassadors that will have polymer activities that meet the National Science Education Standards for K-12.

Science teaching is rewarding, but so is the association with other teachers who share your joy of teaching and learning. While you may feel alone at your school, either because there are no other teachers in your field or because those who are there do not collaborate, there are teachers across the nation (or the world) with whom you can partner.

With a little searching, one can find those individuals who will make your career richer and more fulfilling as science education changes emphasis. Join professional organizations, attend conventions, meet others, share your expertise, and expand your friendships with other professionals. You really might like it!

HELPFUL TIP

Grading notebooks is not a chore! My students are required to keep a notebook for their science class. My goal is to teach organizational skills and help students understand the value of an organized notebook. Having the correct information and being able to find that information when studying for tests, writing laboratory reports, and working on cooperative projects leads to success.

I never collect notebooks for evaluation! I give announced open-notebook (but closed-textbook) quizzes and tests. Periodically I give a five-question quiz that requires the students to find answers to questions in five minutes. I ask questions that reinforce organizational skills. Sample questions and the reasons for the questions are

1. Find the answer to Question 6 from textbook page 55. (Reason: Do they have this homework assignment in their notebook?)

2. What was step three in the procedure to the laboratory on density? (Reason: Do they still have the original laboratory in their possession?)

3. Describe the demonstration that was performed on month/day. (Reason: Did they take notes on this demonstration?)

4. What were the class data for the laboratory on the specific heat of lead? (Reason: Did they write down the class results?)

5. Show your teacher your flashcard on the ammonium ion. (Reason: Have they still got flashcards they were supposed to prepare?)

6. What was the homework assignment for month/day? (Reason: Do they have a syllabus and can they read it correctly?)

Open-notebook tests are 25 questions in 20 minutes. These are announced well in advance so students can prepare if they have not kept their papers organized. Students quickly realize that these grades are an easy way to improve their class average. The open-notebook test in May covers material for the entire semester or year!

I also let students use their notebooks for two minutes toward the end of a closed-book test so that they can find answers to any of the test questions. I do not announce in advance when this opportunity will be offered, so they learn to bring their notebooks to every class. These suggestions for evaluating notebooks for organization and completeness put the burden on the student and not the teacher.

Are We Teaching the Right Things?

GERALD FRIDAY

Milwaukee, Wisconsin

Over the years, one of the major changes in education has been the infusion of environmental education into our curriculum. Breathing clean air, drinking healthy water, and living in balance with our natural environment have become important issues for us.

A question being asked is "Are we teaching environmental education correctly?" One of the criticisms about teaching environmental education is that teachers have a tendency to project their point of view onto their students. Critics feel that the students are actually being brainwashed to think a certain way. This criticism does have some merit because I remember a situation that occurred at an environmental conference I attended with my students.

My high school students had done some water quality testing on a river near our school and had created a presentation to display and explain the data they had gathered. Before our presentation, a group of grade school students, probably in fifth grade, went up to the podium and talked about a lake near their school. They made vague statements and generalizations about how the "water looked polluted."

Upon completion of their presentation, a few other groups, as well as my students, presented their research. The presenters showed tables of data and exhibited graphs that displayed various correlations between the data. Just about the time another group of high school students was about to present its research, the students were whisked away from the podium and replaced with the fifth-grade group that had appeared earlier.

It seems that a news team had arrived to take film footage and the organizers felt the group of younger students would provide more attention to the conference. I wasn't impressed by this move of the organizers. I was actually repulsed by it. I feel these are some of the actions the critics of environmental education are seeing.

My goal in my environmental education course is to try to present material from a scientific framework. Environmental issues that are pertinent to the topics we cover are presented in such a way that both sides are examined. This is accomplished by using a debate format. This results in the discussion of key environmental issues by assigning different sides of the issue. The scientific format also assists the students in developing critical thinking skills as well as the opportunity to develop research skills.

PROCEDURE

In the debate assignment, the class is divided into groups of two students each. The students may select their partner. After brainstorming various environmental issues, both national and local, each two-person team selects an issue and position, pro or con. Teams are then matched with another twosome that is interested in the same issue, but taking an opposing point of view. The groups will have to be somewhat flexible and interested in a number of issues and positions in order to get all the two-student teams matched.

RESEARCH

Our next step is to spend some class time in the school library researching the selected issues and positions. The librarian gives a presentation informing the students as to the various books being held on reserve for them, the location of the vertical file containing news articles that pertain to the selected environmental issues, and how to utilize the library computers for additional information. The library computers are loaded with informative programs on the various environmental issues that have been selected. The computers also allow the students to gather information via the Internet.

The students spend the remainder of the week researching their topics in the library. The library research should provide the students with enough information to successfully debate their issue and write a paper. The paper is easy to write because it is based on the same format as the debate. The paper should actually help the students organize their facts so they can be effectively used in their debate.

A debate calendar is constructed, listing the dates that the various issues will be presented. This calendar is correlated with the units being covered in class.

THE DEBATE

The actual debate should last one entire class period, approximately 50 minutes. The debate begins with an introduction of the topic to be discussed. This takes five minutes, with each team contributing two and a half minutes of the introduction. The purpose of the introduction is to inform the audience what the issue is and explain some background information that will help the audience better understand the debate.

For example, a popular topic is the pros and cons of using sharpshooters to reduce the deer population in our local community. The introduction for this topic would consist of explaining the problem, presenting some of the options to correct the problem, and providing information on the natural history of the deer. Understanding the natural history of the deer helps to explain the reason for a deer population problem.

The introduction is followed with a five-minute presentation by a member of the pro team. This presentation should contain arguments as to why the deer need to be removed and why it should be done by sharpshooters. Factual information should be presented by the speaker.

This presentation is followed by a five-minute address by a member of the con team. This discourse would contain arguments on why the deer need not be removed or, if in agreement, why they must be removed and why sharpshooting is not the way it should be done.

The member of the pro team has two and a half minutes to respond to attacks made by the con presenter, which is followed by the con team also having two and a half minutes to respond to information presented by the pro team. In all, the debate lasts 20 minutes, with each team being responsible for 10 minutes.

For grading purposes, each student must contribute five minutes of information to the debate. This means the primary presenter speaks only once. The student who presents the introduction also handles the closing arguments.

The remainder of the class time is open for questions from the audience directed toward the speakers or a specific team. Members of the audience can ask questions seeking out additional information on the issue being discussed or challenging the presenters on specific points in the debate. My role as moderator is to keep the discussion moving along, not letting any one student dominate the discussion or get into an endless argument.

It is the responsibility of the audience members to understand the issue well enough to be able to write a one-page paper on the debate. They need to take the perspective that they are members of the community's council that will be voting on this issue. Their paper is on which direction they would vote and why they would vote that way.

RESEARCH PAPER

Each team of two students turns in one research paper. The research paper is to model the debate presentation. The goal of the paper is to help organize the students' thoughts before the debate presentation. The student who will be presenting the primary argument is responsible for two pages based on his or her presentation.

The other student in the team writes a one-page introduction and a one-page rebuttal. Both students work on an anticipated offense that they feel will be presented by the opposing team. This paper should be about one page in length. Both students should also construct a bibliography based on the materials they used to research their issue.

HELPFUL TIPS

The students are continually reminded to stay focused on what the issue is about, what the arguments are, what is assumed, and how the arguments are being manipulated. They are shown how to analyze the statements made by various individuals and what those individuals have to gain from their position. The students are also shown how to look for biased language that is being used on both sides of the issue. They are encouraged to research the facts, not the personal opinions on the issue.

As the students do their research, they are requested to be aware of informative charts and graphs that could be used to help make their presentation more informative and persuasive. It is explained and demonstrated that facts become more comprehensible to the audience when they are presented in an organized fashion such as in graphs and charts.

EVALUATION

The paper and presentation are counted as a major test. This is an excellent opportunity for students to shoot for the stars. If students adhere to the format, they should come away with a good grade. Their written paper should portray thorough research, analysis, and organization while the oral debate should demonstrate adequate preparation, analysis, and persuasiveness.

The outcome of the debate has no effect upon the students' grades, but this activity does bring out the competitive spirit of the students. They want the audience to favor their point of view. In adding closure to this activity, after the audience members have written their opinion paper, we vote as to which direction we'll pursue as the governing council.

It is not uncommon for many students to come into the debate with a certain stance, only to change their point of view after hearing the various facts pertaining to the issue. Overall, I feel this is an excellent activity in promoting critical thinking within students and in illustrating the importance of striving for factual information before making decisions.

Let the Science Standards Be Your Guide

VINCENT CARBONE, JR.

Fairfield, Connecticut

My early years as a teacher were exciting and yet frustrating. I began teaching during a time when every curriculum area was being revised and it seemed that more was being added. I needed something to guide my thinking during this time of great change. It was easy to get overwhelmed with all the content. There were a few questions that helped me in my decision making, but I still needed to have some criteria to judge what I was doing.

The National Science Standards helped me answer some of my questions. Some of the questions I grappled with were "What do I want my students to come away with?" and "What do they really need to know?" The standards helped me clarify my thinking. More important, the standards helped me simplify my thinking.

SCIENTIFIC INQUIRY

Scientific investigations may take different forms, including observing what things are like or what is happening somewhere, collecting specimens for analysis, and performing experiments. Students plan and conduct simple investigations. They employ simple equipment and tools to gather data. They use data to construct reasonable explanations.

Students communicate the results of investigations and give explanations. Clear communication is an essential part of doing science.

HABITS OF MIND

Students keep records of their investigations and observations. Students also offer reasons for findings and consider reasons suggested by others.

NATIONAL SCIENCE EDUCATION STANDARDS

The activities investigate and analyze science questions. Learning subject matter disciplines is done in the context of inquiry, technology, and science in personal and social perspectives. There is an integration of all aspects of science content.

TEACHING STANDARDS
EMPHASIZED IN THE SCIENCE PROGRAM

Students are guided in active and extended scientific inquiry. There are many opportunities for scientific discussion and debate among students. Students work with other teachers to enhance the science program. There is a sharing of responsibility for learning among the students. The classroom is a supportive community where cooperation, shared responsibility, and respect are found.

The standards helped me focus on creating a learning environment that was authentic. Process skills would be emphasized in the context of the science content. As the teacher, it is my role to develop the process skills that all scientists use. Therefore, if we were going to study weather, we were going to become meteorologists. If we were going to study the powers that help shape the earth, we were going to become geologists.

My classroom was turned into a geology lab as we studied rocks and minerals collected from a nearby mine. Fossils were sorted and graphed from our second geology trip to the Catskill Mountains in New York State. Scientific groups were set up to study earthquakes and volcanoes. The students downloaded current earthquake and volcano data from the National Earthquake Information Center (www.neic.cr.usgs.gov/currentseismicity.shtml) and from the Update on Current Volcanic Activity (www.volcano.und.edu/vwdocs/current-volcs/current.html).

The students located the earthquakes and volcanoes on a large world map. As they began to plot the data on the map, the students learned firsthand the pattern that created the ring of fire.

The students also worked on projects through KidLink, a global networking for youth (www.kidlink.org). In addition, the Intercultural E-Mail Classroom Connections (IECC) is another global networking opportunity (www.iecc.org).

The projects are wide-ranging. For example, we have participated in a worldwide project on acid rain. Over 250 different classrooms from around the world participated in this unique study of the environment. For a month, each classroom monitored their local rain pH. These data were then shared and analyzed.

Schools communicated with each other as they analyzed and questioned the data. The students have participated on other similar scientific studies—Soil Testing Project, the Water Ways Project, and the Global Sun and Temperature Project.

Students publish their work through an online scientific research journal. The National Student Research Center publishes student research across the K-12 curriculum. It is the first research journal for elementary school students (www.youth.net/nsrc/nsrc.html).

Since I focused on the broader questions and skills, I was freed from having to worry about covering everything in the book. The science book became another sourcebook to consult just like an encyclopedia. The content took care of itself. I was freed up to use my time wisely—doing science.

More important, I was freed up to dream. I wanted to create a classroom that had an authentic feel to whatever we studied. I am currently trying to obtain a seismograph so the students can study earthquake activity as it occurs. The Department of Earth and Atmospheric Sciences at Purdue University has a program for schools to obtain a real seismograph (www.eas/purdue.edu/~braille).

Another primary ingredient to creating an authentic learning environment is to find quality professional development. I believe that every teacher needs to experience a national conference, such as the National Science Teachers Association, at least once in his or her career. In addition, it is important to develop a network of support outside the classroom through conferences, workshops, and coursework.

If it were not for the professional development I participated in, I would never have won the award. A geologist from the local university had a great impact on me. It is because of this connection that my knowledge of earth science grew to the level it is today. We need quality professional development to support the national standards. These go hand-in-hand in making a classroom a place of joy and real learning.

National Academy Press. (1996). *National Science Education Standards*. Washington, DC: Author.

Using Innovations

SHARON JEFFERY

Plymouth, Massachusetts

I am easily bored and so are my students. I believe this is the result of today's fast-moving technological innovations. Brain research has recently shown that people learn new, novel ideas or techniques faster than any other ideas. But I hate the "b-word" and forbid any child to use it in my classroom. I'm always saying, "Boredom is a state of mind and only you are in charge of your mind. Don't tell me you're bored—change your mind!"

However, since I am in charge of my instruction techniques I go out of my way to vary them with each unit I teach. The science department in the Plymouth Public Schools is led by a wonderful "idea" man who is always networking with technology providers and teaching institutes to provide us with state-of-the-art teaching opportunities.

We were the first school system around to get our district curriculum on the Web. We pilot new science toys and tools every year. We teachers are encouraged to try anything that seems logical. Active research is encouraged. Professional development courses over the past few years have included learning numerous computer programs to enhance teaching and student learning.

I use my summers to attend conferences to update myself in terms of technology and pedagogy. These include everything from small, free, local events to nationwide six-week courses to international virtual learning courses. These all provide me with new ideas to be used in the classroom to enliven the learning.

Web searches provide me with an abundance of ideas. I jump at every chance to participate in Internet learning with my students. The more realistic the student learning is, the more likely the students are to actually learn. We have exchanged data on shadow lengths, tessellated quilts, marble rolling, genetic traits, local wildlife, and weather factors.

I will try almost anything once to see how it will work for me in my classroom. Some ideas take so much time they aren't practical, but I can modify them to be more useful. I don't keep all these findings to myself. I share these with my fellow teachers on a one-to-one basis, at Open House night with parents, or at presentations through state conferences.

Using these innovations means more work and more time invested in getting ready for my classroom. I believe it is time well spent. I thrive on having students tell me they look forward to getting to class every day just to see what we are going to do. Student surveys have consistently reported they love the idea that they never know what we are going to do. But before you get the idea my classroom is a free-for-all, this is all done in the context of some unswerving class management schemes.

This year one of the new innovations I tried out was Webquests. These open-ended learning experiences allow students to choose a specific question on a given topic, which they investigate online. They then share their results with others via a Web site or PowerPoint presentation. Students loved these experiences since they could investigate an area that interested them specifically.

I endeavor to make learning seem like playtime. Having taught preschool for many years, I know that young children need to play to learn. When do you stop being a child? Certainly my 13-year-old eighth graders love to play—heck, I still do as I approach my half-century mark. If I can make learning fun I bet lots more of it will happen! Since today's play includes much more technology, that must be considered when designing classroom instruction.

A New Teaching Innovation

GERALD FRIDAY

Milwaukee, Wisconsin

I love teaching. I especially enjoy teaching when students grasp a concept I'm trying to relate. You could say their comprehension provides the adrenaline that gets me excited. For me, this is the motivation that results in my putting in the extra time by reading educational journals and attending convention workshops to find new and innovative ways of getting my students to learn.

When attending recent workshops, I've noticed the ideas presented to me are concepts that I've heard or used before but the language or terminology is new. For example, when I started teaching 37 years ago, I taught my biology students by using inquiry learning. This was a method that consisted of students learning through their own discovery.

Back then, their discovery was acquired through lab activities that were followed with class discussions in which students shared information and ideas learned from the activities. Today I engage in the same approach, except now, besides the lab activities, I'm likely to also incorporate computer and library activities and replace some of the class discussions with student presentations. When I describe my approach to younger teachers, I'm less likely to call it "inquiry learning" than "student-centered learning."

So for me, has teaching changed? Probably not a lot, other than the increased use of computer and library activities. But that was during my first 32 years of teaching. The past five years have really changed for me. It was during these past five years that I was introduced to environmental education. Environmental education is unique in that it is based on wonderful methodology. In this methodology, students are first made aware of a concept or issue. They next acquire knowledge to thoroughly understand the concept. They then take action to actually incorporate their new awareness and knowledge into their lives. It's this last step in this process that has me so excited.

An example demonstrating how this methodology works is through an activity that we do as part of my science club. This club consists of a group of students who are extremely interested in science and the environment. After reading and listening to our local news, we had heard that our community was very poor at recycling. It was actually found that the compliance rate of recycling within our community was about 25%, while in the outlying municipalities the rate was about 95%. We discussed this issue and decided to make our community more aware of the recycling issue by providing them with a knowledge of recycling and getting them to take action, to recycle.

We were already aware of the issue. We next needed to acquire knowledge about recycling. This was accomplished by the students dividing the special areas of recycling (paper, plastic, steel, rubber, etc.) and each student researching an area. Letters were written to companies and organizations requesting additional information or materials that would help us understand the recycling process.

The response from the letters resulted in our receiving sample materials ranging from recycled rubber mats to plastics in various stages of being recycled. Our newly acquired knowledge and materials led us to believe that the best course of action for us to take was to create a recycling show that could be presented to grade school students. It was our goal to make them aware of recycling, increase their knowledge of recycling, and motivate them to actively recycle.

Our recycling show has become very popular in our community. Over the years we have traveled to grade schools presenting our show and have even had grade school students come to our school to see our show. Recently, the show has become so popular that the students have been performing at museums and fairs.

The students are continually making the show better by adding new information and demonstrations. The students have even created special characters wearing costumes to portray the various recycling experts: the scientist, the forester, the steelworker, and the worm farmer.

The recycling show is a great activity and a wonderful example of how the environmental education methodology works, but I feel this methodology also can be used in other disciplines. In my area of biology, I visualize my students being made aware of heart disease, gathering and sharing knowledge relative to heart disease, and then creating an action plan to do something about it. An action plan may consist of encouraging our cafeteria staff to create a heart-friendly menu, or a plan could provide blood pressure testing at our school for the community. Oh, if I could just teach for another 37 years!

When the Unthinkable Happens: Teachers Talk About September 11, 2001

Thoughts on September 11th

CARMELLA ETTARO

West Hills, California

I was getting ready for school, listening to the news when the first plane hit. At first I thought it was an accident. Being in California and up at 5:00 a.m. because I have students arriving at 6:30 a.m. for a 7:00 a.m. class, by the time I drove the 15 miles to the school, all the while listening to the news, I knew this was not an accident.

My television in the classroom doesn't work, so a colleague found me in his room riveted to his set. He didn't know what had happened. He is the first person I told about what happened. It was so strange to talk about it. Somehow, it didn't seem real. He got my television working just as another teacher came running down the hall saying the Pentagon was hit.

I had the television on as students came in. Some knew, while others wondered what was going on. Going through my mind was that I am the adult. How was I going to deal with the students when I was so afraid of the terrorist nature of this attack? What about my Middle Eastern students who are innocents in this and must be protected from unwarranted discrimination? What must the Persian teacher in my department be feeling? I wanted to be sensitive to them and needed to model this for my students.

I try to always be honest with students and answer their questions. That day I let them set the pace of how they wanted to deal with what happened. I feel students need to see teachers as human beings, who don't know all the answers and who can share feelings of both happiness and sadness. My students know when I say oops after making a mistake, get excited about learning something new, or talk about the beauty of some math concept that I am sincere.

I let them see me, the person inside the teacher. The stereotypical (female) math teacher is not what my students get in my classroom. We saw many of that terrible day's events live. They heard my gasp when the buildings collapsed. I didn't hide my emotions. I did turn the television off to teach.

I felt the students needed to have some normal routine that day, but if they asked, I did turn it back on. I let some of my third-period students meet with others in the hallway to pray for the victims. I felt students needed to have some control over their feelings of helplessness.

It seemed important to let them have some say in how to handle this day. In talking with other teachers, many tried to provide a sense of security for their students, while knowing their future had been changed. Some students did not feel enough was done and thought, by teaching that day, teachers showed insensitivity to the tragedy of the events. Other students were grateful to escape into their studies and not listen to the (repetitive) news reports.

By modeling behavior of seeking answers and talking with others for support, I hope to give my students coping skills for life's ups and downs and help them through other difficult times that will come into their lives. In the days that followed, students had a need to contribute something. A teddy bear drive was organized, T-shirts were sold, and flowers were set out by the flagpole.

Kindergartners Face the Tragic Day

MICHELLE MASH

Wilmington, Delaware

There I sat on the playground bench watching my little kindergartners. Some were swinging, sliding, and playing tag and some were hanging out with me sharing life's important thoughts. Our vice principal came out and asked to speak to us privately. Just then, in her tone, we heard that something was seriously wrong. She explained to us what had happened in New York City. It seemed so surreal.

As a teacher I feel so out of touch with what is happening in the world. We are so isolated in our day with limited adult contact, let alone contact with worldly events. Even though recess was not over I felt a sense of urgency to get the children inside where it was safe. The staff was told at this time we were not to tell the children anything but to continue on as if it was a normal day.

As a kindergarten teacher and a mother I felt very strongly that parents should be the ones to explain the events to their child. Each parent has a different approach. Some would tell the minimal amount of news while some would allow their child to sit in front of the television and listen and see as much news as possible.

As I was reading aloud to my little ones I was interrupted again with the news that I was to prepare to exit the building as we had just received a bomb threat. Trying not to show emotion I had the children line up with their things and we proceeded outside. The children were confused because it was close to dismissal. They saw the buses and yet their teacher was not putting them on the bus.

They were quick to see the police cars and bomb-sniffing dogs and had many questions that I could not answer because I, too, was waiting for information. After receiving word to dismiss my morning children I put them on the buses and sent my walkers with their parents, who shared the insights of the tragic news with me.

The next day, feeling quite empty and drained, we returned to school. It was decided that we would discuss the happenings in our school and around our world in our class-room. I asked the guidance counselor to come into my room to assist. My class began the discussion by telling what they knew. Many were as concerned about the bomb scare as I was.

I gave the children a fair amount of time to allow each child to discuss what was on his or her mind. I saw the children respond in many different ways. Some participated in the discussion. Others wrote tiny books about the events as they understood them. Many built towers replicating the twin towers in the block center.

I allowed the children several different opportunities to express their feelings and to validate their thoughts as they shared during our center share time. Our school is very com-munity centered and we quickly collected things to be sent up to New York to help.

The children were eager to show the items that they were donating to the cause. Five-year-olds have a voice and need to be heard. By validating and truly listening to my young students I foster their self-esteem and learning.

The Power of Dialogue

MARY DANEELS

West Chicago, Illinois

In my first year of teaching, one of my students was killed in a tragic car accident. I turned to my mentor for advice as to how to handle the situation. Should I go on with the lesson plan, avoid the situation and provide the students an "escape" from the tragedy, or address it in class, and if so, how?

He counseled me to address the circumstances, share my feelings with the class, and create a safe environment for the kids to share their emotions and thoughts. It was a heart-wrenching class, painful but cathartic.

After that class, we knew that we were not alone in our feelings of grief over our loss, confusion about how such a thing could happen, and uncertainty about our own mortality. I learned an important lesson that day about the power of dialogue and how it could bring people together and promote respect.

Dr. Maslow's "Hierarchy of Needs" taught us that people do not learn (self-actualize) until their need for safety is met. The events of September 11, 2001, shook everyone's perception of the world around them to the core. To go on with the lesson plan that day would have been absurd.

The students had questions and I did not have all of the answers, but I could provide a safe environment for them to share their thoughts, dispel myths, and learn from the tragic events as they unfolded. I could give them unconditional acceptance, no matter what their fears were. Their classmates could listen and let them know that they were not alone.

Ralph Nader stated, "Information is the currency of democracy." In these trying times, I feel it is my responsibility as a teacher to model and encourage civil discourse in my classroom about the current War on Terrorism. An informed citizen is crucial to our nation's strength and survival. Civil discourse among citizens is key in that it promotes listening to one another, the exchange of ideas, and most of all, understanding.

By engaging in civil discourse, students help one another sort out fact from fiction, identify bias and misperceptions, and seek out answers in a safe environment that lets them know that they are not alone in these troubling times. A friend stated that we as educators are to be "ambassadors of reason."

Sometimes, our discussions get a bit heated in class and disagreements occur. In these situations, my role as ambassador is a bit tricky. I know in the end, by practicing civil discourse, students learn to be in opposition to ideas, not people, and that it is okay to agree to disagree.

Students learn to listen and empathize with one another and walk away knowing that a person isn't "evil" just because he or she has a different perception of the world. I think this is an important lesson for teachers to convey to their students today. Wouldn't it be a better world if everyone could learn that lesson?

Helping Students Cope

LLOYD BARBER

Evanston, Illinois

Developmentally, first-grade students are oftentimes unclear when it comes to distinguishing between fact and fantasy. Their words and thoughts are mixed between what they actually know and what they sometimes construct in their minds. After the events of September 11th, I spent several days working with the students in my classroom on these differences.

Many children today watch television news and somewhat violent shows or movies. These children, of course, saw the news that followed the events of September 11th and thought that it was simply another movie or show similar to one that they had seen before. I tried to explain to them that these clips that they had seen were, in fact, real and perpetrated by people who did not understand our country or our people.

We talked about how people are different in terms of color, religion, ethnicity, socioeconomic status, and gender. Using these differences as a base, we broadened our discussion to include nations of other people who do not understand our nation. I also included a discussion of how our nation and culture does not always understand the culture of another nation. We concluded the discussion with talking about the importance of always listening to others and respecting their differences.

As a follow-up to these discussions, I read *Oliver Button Is a Sissy* by Tomie dePaola and *William's Doll* by Charlotte Zolotow. These two books are excellent examples of the importance of respecting the rights of others. In addition, they teach both children and adults the much-needed quality of tolerance.

Care for Our Children

PERCY HILL

Andover, New Hampshire

On the morning of September 12, 2001, a second-grade boy came to me and asked if I had seen that "terrible thing" that happened on television yesterday. It was understood that the entire staff of our small K-8 school remained mute throughout the horror that took place on September 11th. That young boy had no way of knowing what his teachers struggled through Tuesday to be prepared for the questions and sorrows that were to follow on Wednesday.

I often wonder how any of us even functioned during the day as we received bits and pieces of information and updates of the absolute horror that was taking place in our backyard. The staff joined together to offer strength and wisdom for what was to follow: care for our children.

The second grader went on to exclaim, "Mr. Hill, I've been thinking. When I saw the people jumping from those tall buildings, we could have saved them if we had only put trampolines all around for the people to land on!" I agreed and told him how proud I was of his dear thoughtfulness and concern for life. Moments later, an eighth-grade girl approached me with tears in her eyes. She asked how and why anyone could do such a thing to innocent people. I realized that these children had never before experienced such terror and waste of human life.

I would have to dig deep into my own knowledge and wisdom to respond appropriately to all of the comments, questions, and concerns that I was about to face. This child was suddenly faced with real inner conflict regarding justice and value of human life.

Just yesterday, her greatest worry was whether or not she would be invited to the first dance of the school year. Her closing remarks painted a picture colored with sadness. She told me that she didn't know any of the victims, but she prayed for them and cried. She went on to say, "I hope we catch the people that did this. They deserve to die. Is it wrong for me to feel like that?"

Those were just two of the many children I spoke with following the horrific tragedy of September 11, 2001. The children's emotions ranged from sadness to anger and from concern to fear; all were feeling displaced and uncertain about their own safety and the security of their families and loved ones. Many of the children asked if we were all going to die!

Our staff worked diligently to maintain our own silence and composure during the school day on September 11th. We all agreed that we should say nothing and offer "no news" on that day. It was also agreed that the first news of the tragedy should come from their families and loved ones. The entire staff of our small New Hampshire public school would join together as a crisis team to begin on September 12th to go as far as the children needed and for as long as they wanted.

Each and every teacher opened his or her classroom and heart to help guide the children through this most difficult time. Our middle school social studies teacher brought news articles to the classroom each day to help the children make some sense of the day-to-day happenings. We made ourselves available to listen and let the children know that we care and to offer support, security, and love. We gave them little advice, but encouraged them to speak from their hearts. There were no right or wrong feelings and no right or wrong answers. Only the words that came from their innocence and youthful wisdom were honest and correct.

During the days that followed September 11th, the children redirected their focus to concerns for the victims and families of the tragedy. The students were reacting to feelings of helplessness and were asking for ways that they could help. Our school nurse, a staff member, and I organized a school- and community-wide penny drive to present funds to the American Red Cross Relief Fund.

All of the children and many community members contributed to the cause by bringing in containers of pennies to deposit at the base of our American flag. We placed the tribute of Red, White, and Blue in the center of the gymnasium and watched with tearful emotion as the children, class by class, deposited their tokens of faith and healing. Our ceremony was brief, pictures were taken, and words were said. Everyone joined in the singing of "God Bless America." It was very clear that we felt every word.

As we attempt to put September 11th behind us, we still have many questions unanswered, questions that will probably never be fully answered. But we must always remember to teach about peace in the form of love and the highest value for life

September 11, 2001—"It's No Movie"

SHARON JEFFERY

Plymouth, Massachusetts

On September 11, 2001, I was in the middle of a teacher meeting in my classroom when another staff member popped in to tell us to turn on the news. She was crying so we envisioned some assassination or natural disaster. I turned on the television. To our horror we watched as a plane hit the second tower. We sat dumbfounded, wondering what was going on. For 10 minutes the dozen people in my room sat in silence—eyes glued to the screen. I spent the time praying silently for our leaders and military.

When the bell rang I decided instantaneously to shut the television off. Why? I didn't know right then, but later I realized I felt the parents had the right to inform their children. I had no answers to give them, so why give them the information? But I soon thought they would go home to empty houses, turn on the news, and be shocked. It was a dilemma—one that teaching school can't prepare you for.

One young boy came in just as I was shutting off the television. He looked at it and said, "Cool! What movie is this?" I simply stated, "It's no movie." I then proceeded to teach as though things were normal. My mind was reeling about what to do—so I pretended it hadn't happened.

When my last class came in after lunch things were totally different. They had been told what was going on at lunch. They now knew of the other two planes and the fact that this was a planned attack. Many students were visibly upset and unable to concentrate. Dozens of parents had dismissed their children in order to have them at home. Some were dismissed because their parents had been activated and would be leaving with a military group.

Rumors and truth flew equally. I found it hard to concentrate and justify teaching about water conservation when our future was so shaky. I scrapped my lesson and allowed the children to talk about their feelings. I expressed my concerns about who was responsible and wondered if anything else was going to happen. Most were wondering if the nuclear power plant down the street was a likely target. Students asked if the bad guys were still in Boston and how many people had died in the collapsing towers.

Science teachers are not used to not having the answers. It was a tough day that became a tough week that lingers still.

Not Another Normal Day

VINCENT CARBONE, JR.

Fairfield, Connecticut

There are two days I felt totally unprepared for in my career—the events at Columbine High School and the events of September 11th. I had great difficulty accepting the images and reports from my computer that awful morning of the 11th.

My principal called me and another teacher out of our classes to break the news. She gave us specific instructions not to tell the children what was going on. Our job was to provide a safe, calm environment. She expected parents to come to the school to pick up their children—especially those families whose parents worked in the city. After school the entire staff was going to meet to plan for the next day. We did not even know if we were going to have school the next day.

At first I felt this sense of chaos. The two towers were hit, the Pentagon was hit, and a plane was down in Pennsylvania. The President was somewhere between Florida and Washington. Two surrounding towns immediately canceled school for the rest of the day. I was wondering if anything else was going to happen. I thought of the children in my school.

Many of their mothers and fathers commute from Fairfield, Connecticut, to New York City for work. I also thought of some of the staff whose spouses worked in the city.

One of my colleagues got a call from her daughter who attends college in the city. She called in hysterics describing how she saw the towers come down. Her father works in one of the towers. Luckily her father was at a meeting in another part of town that day. While all this was going on, I was supposed to teach as though this was a normal day.

Some parents came to pick up their children. A few parents came with the intention of picking their children up but when they saw the school environment was in total peace, they turned around and went back home. I credit my principal for her quick decision not to deal with the situation as it was unfolding. We left it up to the families to first deal with this event with their children.

After the staff met to discuss how we would deal with the next day, we all braced for the worst. How many of our families were going to be affected? We were fortunate to find that none of the families were directly affected. On the other hand, we all knew of someone who was affected.

I have a friend whose sister was on the 96th floor of Tower One. The mood around the building before school was quiet and stressed. We all were still in a great deal of shock. I had great difficulty concentrating and so did others. I wondered if I was going to make it through the day. How was I going to go through a normal day? What was I going to say to the children?

The children came in on the 12th very talkative. I sat at my desk and allowed them extra time to talk with their friends. Every adult needed to talk about these events so I figured they did too. I felt very sad that these kids had to witness these kinds of events. I felt their innocence was taken from them.

It was interesting watching their conversations. They were discussing the events as if it was a movie—sort of detached. I was relieved for this. We spoke briefly about the events and I tried to continue with school as normal as possible.

It was not until I received a homework assignment a few days later that I saw a better picture of how they were really thinking. On the 14th I received their spelling sentences. Most of them put their spelling words in sentences dealing with the events of the 11th. I couldn't read through them so I threw them out.

In the weeks that followed the students continued to use their spelling sentences to talk about the events of the 11th. As a school we participated in the "Pledge Across America." This gave me a great opportunity to talk about the words of the pledge in more detail.

My classroom subscribes to *Time for Kids* magazine. I was worried about how they were going to deal with the events of the 11th, the war in Afghanistan, and the anthrax problem. So far the magazine has given me a chance to discuss these things with them. Out of all the things we did as a school, I believe the decision to keep the school environment safe and secure on the 11th was the wisest.

I cannot imagine the chaos that went through the children's minds those first few days after the 11th. I believe that having school on the 12th and continuing on with business as usual sent an important message to the students. It gave them back a sense of order in the midst of the chaos.

September 11, 2001: Reaction

Steven T. Jackson

Harrisonburg, Virginia

September 9, 2001, was a day of celebration for our school. After a long and arduous 3.1 million dollar renovation, it was a day of rededication to the community for our school. One of the invited guests was Spotswood Elementary School's first principal (1960 to 1964). In his remarks he talked of joys of the job and challenges. He talked about a Friday in November of 1963 when they heard that President John F. Kennedy had died. The entire school met around the flagpole at the end of the day for a moment of silence.

His words were still ringing in our heads when news was breaking all day on the 11th. As teachers took their students to lunch, I informed them that they might want to watch television coverage unfolding during their break. Around noon, we had three or four parents who showed up to take their children home. In each case, I asked them why. Most of them felt their children were not safe at school.

I disagreed with them and told them their children would be better off having a "business as usual" day. In each case, the parent agreed. (I have been at this school for 12 years and have built a great trust with our parents and community.) We met as a staff at the end of the day and discussed how we should handle the situation.

It was decided that we would open up discussion at the beginning of each day for the remainder of the week. Students would lead the discussion and teachers would guide them. Our counselor would be on call for any students displaying extreme concerns or questions. The week went as well as could be expected. We did not experience any increase in absenteeism. One of our parents works in the Pentagon and got out before the fireball engulfed his office.

That Friday was designated by local government as a Day of Patriotism in the Valley. We asked each student to wear red, white, and blue. To our astonishment, all of our students participated. Thirty-eight percent of our students speak English as a second language and 14 different languages are spoken at our school.

One of our kindergarten teachers asked if we could have our state mandate a moment of silence at noon around the flagpole. The teacher said he kept thinking about what the former principal had said and thought it would be appropriate that when our nation was in prayer, we would be too.

The entire school shut down for 10 minutes while students filed out of classrooms and others left their lunches in the cafeteria for our Pledge and a moment of silence. Our fifth graders recited the Preamble to the Constitution. It was a very touching moment for our school. Also on Friday, I wrote our staff a letter thanking them for their diligence and professionalism throughout the week. I stated that people in other professions could watch television and be updated constantly. In other professions, offices closed, but we continued to teach and lead.

Our school had two direct outcomes from that fateful day in September. The first was a penny drive in which we collected 54,904 pennies, which were donated to the victims. The second was a partnership with PS 150 in Manhattan. This school had to be evacuated because of air quality concerns. It was relocated to PS 3 along with two other schools.

After consultation with PS 150's principal, we decided to donate all of our proceeds from our fourth annual chili cook-off to the teachers of PS 150. Each of the eight teachers received $70 for anything they wished. We told them that we were touched by the events of September 11, 2001, and that our thoughts and prayers were with them. We wanted the money to go to their classroom, to their students, or even for the teacher to go out to dinner. Each of the classroom teachers was touched by our donations. We have received numerous cards and letters of appreciation.

Index

**CORWIN
PRESS**

The Corwin Press logo—a raven striding across an open book—represents the happy union of courage and learning. We are a professional-level publisher of books and journals for K-12 educators, and we are committed to creating and providing resources that embody these qualities. Corwin's motto is "Success for All Learners."